Listen to Ngarrindjeri Women Speaking

Kungun Ngarrindjeri Miminar Yunnan

*S*PINIFEX PRESS

Spinifex Press Pty Ltd
504 Queensberry Street
North Melbourne, Vic 3051
women@spinifexpress.com.au
http://www.spinifexpress.com.au

First published by Spinifex Press, 2008

Cover design Deb Snibson with Aunty Ellen Trevorrow and *Ngarrindjeri Miminar*
Typeset by Emma Statham
Printed by McPherson's Printing Group
Index by Diane Bell and Claire Simmonds

National Library of Australia
Cataloguing-in-Publication entry:
    Bell, Diane, 1943-
    Listen to Ngarrindjeri Women Speaking/Kungun Ngarrindjeri Miminar Yunnan

    ISBN: 9781876756697
    1. Ngarrindjeri (Australian people)–Social life and customs. 2. Women, Aboriginal Australian–
    South Australia–Social life and customs. 3. Oral tradition–South Australia. 4. Storytelling–
    South Australia. 5. Hindmarsh Island (S. Aust.)–Social life and customs. I. Title

    305.89915

This publication is assisted by the Office of Indigenous Policy Coordination, Department of Families,
Housing, Community Services and Indigenous Affairs and Country Arts SA.

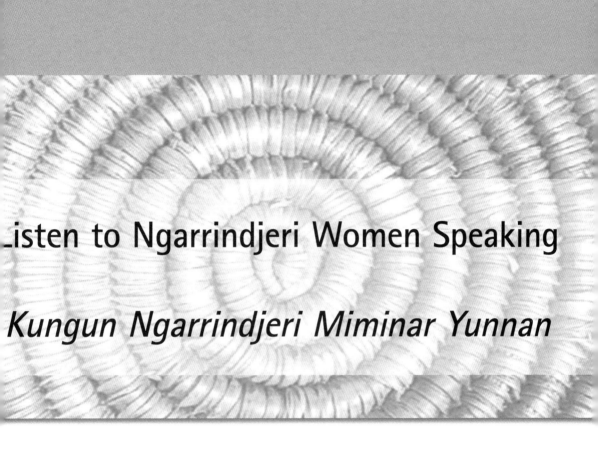

Listen to Ngarrindjeri Women Speaking

Kungun Ngarrindjeri Miminar Yunnan

edited by
Diane Bell
for the Ngarrindjeri Nation
2008

SPINIFEX PRESS

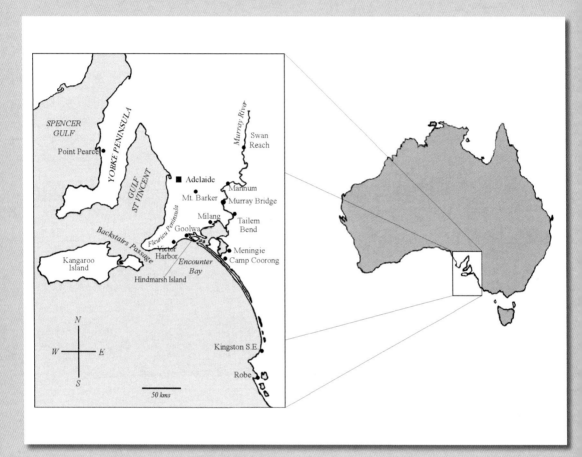

Location Map

Dedication

To all Ngarrindjeri, past, present and future.

Our respect for all living things

and our fight for Truth, Justice and Equity within our Lands and Waters

guides us Ngarrindjeri *miminar* in the development of our plans.

May our Spirits find rest and peace within our Lands and Waters.

Table of Contents

Prologue

Miminar Thunggalun Yunti
Women Standing Together

What are our needs?[1]

What do we want to address our needs?

Where are we going?

What does the future hold for us, our children,
our grandchildren, our young women?

Namawi rawul-inyeri thulun-ar. Our footprints [come] from the past. From our ancestors to us, we are the traditional owners, still guiding our young ones, connecting the Stolen Generations back to family and country, standing strong in our history and culture and heritage.

Us women who are writing this Prologue are a group of strong-minded Ngarrindjeri *miminar* [women], young and old, who have had enough of this system of things. We're tired of always having to explain our existence and to prove our Aboriginality.

These are our words: our stories.

The stories of our Elders are a constant reminder of our Law and how we are related to the land, our *ngatji* [totems] and to each other.

The focus of our *ruwi* [country] is the land and waters of the River, Lakes and Coorong and Encounter Bay.

Our history since contact with *kringkarar* [non-Indigenous people] has been one of oppression, theft of land and children, destruction of our lands, waters and sacred places, of forbidding language use, and dispossession. However, despite our families being broken up and our children stolen, we are determined to stay strong as the Ngarrindjeri Nation. In the face of all the intrusions and interventions and attacks on our culture, we are here today. We never left our country. We are caring for it still.

This book is about our country, story-telling, weaving, painting, family, law, culture, history, and government. It's about the past, present and future.

In the past, many of us were forced to become 'fringe dwellers' around the towns that grew up in our traditional land. It wasn't our choice. Some of us were moved onto missions like Raukkan [Point McLeay]. If we lived off the mission we had to get permission to visit our families on the mission, even as recently as 1972. Government policies restricted our access to our own country and the practice of our traditional culture. They divided families. The policy of assimilation told us to be like whites, and they forced their values on us. We reckon we must be a really talented and intelligent people to have held onto our own values and culture and also to have learned theirs.

Through working on this book, we've told our stories and talked about our priorities. We've enjoyed coming down here to Camp Coorong for the workshops, sharing our stories – we sort of lose connection and it's been good reconnecting. It's moving the younger ones forward. We're trying to bring people in.

Today our struggles continue. We are still being asked to prove ourselves. We are having to argue over and over again that we want our places to be safe. We want healthy country and healthy bodies. We don't want our sites destroyed, the land and water and air polluted. The increased salinity in the River and Lakes is killing our *ngatji* [totems]. The pollution is killing us.

Racism, ignorance and denial persist. We face racism in everyday life – direct, indirect and institutionalised racism – in education, with the police, in health care, in housing, employment and even in sport. Racial stereotypes and taunts hurt us but we are working to raise our self-esteem and confidence and to strengthen our Ngarrindjeri identity.

The government talks about our welfare but their words don't match their deeds. We see the criminal justice system taking violence against our women less seriously than for other women. And what about drugs and alcohol and pornography? Who is getting rich on those things? Who brought these poisons into our country?

The genocide continues.

We're looking to the future. We're establishing a foundation for the continuity and sustainability of our culture, for the benefit of our future generations. Instead of our *miwi* [inner spirit] grieving, we are determined that it will rejoice and we can return to being a happy nation again.

We asked Professor Diane Bell to help us with the research and editing and we gave her an exemption certificate[2] because she accepted us. We see this kind of writing as a positive step towards reconciliation, in breaking down barriers, and an example of Aboriginal and non-Aboriginal people working together.

Our hopes are that everyone will read this book and have a better and more accurate idea of who we are, what we do and what we care about.[3]

Alice Abdulla, Edie Carter, Vicki Hartman, Helen Jackson, Innes Jackson, Audrey Lindsay, Rita Lindsay Jr, Donna Kartinyeri, Dorothy Kartinyeri, Noreen Kartinyeri, Rita Lindsay, Thelma Smart, Ellen Trevorrow, Georgina Trevorrow, Eileen McHughes, Phyllis Williams.

Camp Coorong, August 19, 2007

Acknowledgements

Kungun Ngarrindjeri Miminar Yunnan is a weave of voices, ideas, texts, images and strategies and we are grateful to all who offered advice, shared stories and photographs, posed questions, emailed responses, contributed drawings and took notes. Thanks to all the Ngarrindjeri women and children who participated in the workshops at Camp Coorong in 2007: Aunty Alice Abdulla, Aunty Eunice Aston, Jessie Aston, Cheyeanne Carter, Edie Carter, Julie Carter, Aunty Hilda Day, Aunty Margaret Dodd, Aunty Vicki Hartman, Aunty Helen Jackson, Innes Jackson, Donna Kartinyeri, Dorothy Kartinyeri, Aunty Noreen Kartinyeri, Phoebe Kartinyeri, Aunty Rita Lindsay, Audrey Lindsay, Rita Lindsay Jr, Harmony Love, Latoya Love, Aunty Eileen McHughes, Vicki Miller, Kaitlin Reid, Bessie Rigney, Aunty Innes Rigney, Aunty Millie Rigney, Aunty Dorothy Shaw, Aunty Thelma Smart, Aunty Adeline Smith, Kaysha Taylor, Aunty Ellen Trevorrow, Georgia Trevorrow, Georgie Trevorrow, Georgina Trevorrow, Jasmine Trevorrow, Aunty Shirley Trevorrow, Aunty Phyllis Williams, Aunty Glenys Wilson and special thanks to the kitchen crew at Camp Coorong who kept us fed.

Thanks to Diane Bell, University of Adelaide and Flinders University; Shaun Berg and Claire Simmonds, Hunt and Hunt, Adelaide; Mary-Anne Gale, University of Adelaide; Steve Hemming, Flinders University; Anne McMahon, Lower Murray Nungas Club, Community Services Program, Murray Bridge; Vesper Tjukonai, Narrung; and Annie Vanderwyk, Newcastle University for their thoughtful contributions. Thanks to the individual photographers and artists as acknowledged throughout the text.

Thanks to Uncle Tom Trevorrow (Chairperson) and Aunty Ellen Trevorrow (Treasurer) of the Ngarrindjeri Land and Progress Association (NLPA) Inc. for initiating the project and seeing it through. We plan to distribute *Kungun Ngarrindjeri Miminar Yunnan* throughout the Ngarrindjeri Nation and are pleased that, with Spinifex Press as a partner, the book will also reach a broader Australian and international reading public. Thanks to the creative team at Spinifex Press, in particular publishers Susan Hawthorne and Renate Klein, Deb Snibson and Emma Statham for design work and typesetting and Belinda Morris for her editing.

Finally, thanks to the Indigenous Women's Leadership Program, Office of Indigenous Policy Coordination (OIPC), Department of Families, Housing, Community Services and Indigenous Affairs (FaHCSIA) for their funding of the workshops and contribution to the costs of printing and to Country Arts SA for their assistance via a Quick Response Grant.

Our Workshops — Our Book

In June 2007, the invitations from the Ngarrindjeri Land and Progress Association (NLPA) Inc. went out: Ngarrindjeri women are urged to attend a workshop to discuss (1) the newly formed Ngarrindjeri Regional Authority Inc. and (2) the Ngarrindjeri partnership arrangements with the Federal and State Governments for Caring for Country and Economic Developments. Aunty Ellen Trevorrow, as the NLPA Treasurer, had successfully sought funding from the Indigenous Women's Leadership Program to conduct two weekend workshops at Camp Coorong, near Meningie in South Australia. She invited Diane Bell to facilitate the workshops. Within a week we began our work.

Day One: Camp Coorong June 23, 2007

Back row: Kaitlin Reid, Georgie Trevorrow, Rita Lindsay, Ellen Trevorrow, Thelma Smart, Eileen McHughes, Vicki Hartman, Margaret Dodd, Helen Jackson, Shirley Trevorrow, Noreen Kartinyeri, Annie Vanderwyk

Front row: Georgina Trevorrow, Donna Kartinyeri, Dorothy and Phoebe Kartinyeri, Alice Abdulla, Anne McMahon, Diane Bell   Photograph: Diane Bell

There was so much to do and so much to be said. We learned many things as we shared stories, asked questions, listened, laughed and cried. The two workshops became four. We met with the men to hear more of their plans for the Ngarrindjeri Regional Authority Inc. (NRA). We read *Yarluwar-Ruwe Plan*, the book that sets out the Sea-Country Plan for the Ngarrindjeri Nation and are pleased to add more of our stories to the Plan.[4] We read ethnographic and historical accounts of Ngarrindjeri culture and talked about legal documents concerning our rights as parents, as the traditional owners of Ngarrindjeri *ruwi* [country] and as members of the Ngarrindjeri Nation. We continued the conversations about caring for country, our families, and our nation by telephone, email and text. More meetings. We read and reread drafts, added more stories. We had a book. We explained our Ngarrindjeri way of using respect terms like Aunty and Uncle and how we wanted to spell Ngarrindjeri words to Diane. That's all in the Epilogue where she talks more about the workshops, the research, writing and rewriting process.

Workshop Activities, Camp Coorong,
June 23–4, 2007

Photo 1. Donna Kartinyeri
Photo 2. Thelma Smart and Helen Jackson
Photo 3. Margaret Dodd and Ellen Trevorrow
Photographs: Annie Vanderwyk

Caring for Country

There is a whole ritual in weaving, from where we actually start, the centre part of the piece, you're creating loops to weave into, then you move into the circle. You keep going round and round creating the loops and once the children do those stages they're talking, actually having a conversation, just like our Old People. It's sharing time. And that's where our stories are told.

Aunty Ellen Trevorrow 2007

I'm lucky I can talk with the older ones, but I know others missed out.

Edie Carter 2007

All we need is in our stories

How are stories told? Who gets to tell them? Who gets to listen? What happens when the spoken word is written down and may reach a wider audience, an audience not necessarily bound by the cultural rules of the story-teller? Ngarrindjeri take their stories seriously. Stories sustain and structure the Ngarrindjeri social world; explain the mysterious; provide a secure haven in an otherwise hostile world; bring order to and confer significance on relationships amongst the living; hold hope for future generations; and open up communication with those who have passed on. Stories of cultural life recall the creation of the land, of the seas, rivers, lakes and lagoons. They tell of the differentiation of species and of languages. They spell out the proper uses of flora and fauna. These are stories of human frailty and triumph, of deception and duty, of rights, responsibilities and obligations, of magical beings, creative heroes and destructive forces. Everything has a story, but not everyone knows every story. Nor does everyone have the right to hear every story, or having heard it, to repeat the words.[5]

In many diverse ways, some highly visible, some almost invisible, Ngarrindjeri women and men care for country. This care is all part of being proud of Ngarrindjeri culture, past, present and future. Knowing the stories, passing on the stories and being a story-teller are ways that Ngarrindjeri care for country. This is what Ngarrindjeri *miminar* [women] had to say:

> We have to keep our culture alive.
>
> We want access to our special places, our lands and our waters.
>
> We need to be able to protect our places, our *ngatji* [totems], our Old People and restore damaged sites.
>
> We want respect for our land and our water and we want to pass down knowledge.

Respect is a core Ngarrindjeri value: respect for country, stories, the Elders, the Old People who have passed away. The respect system sets out the proper way of behaving: it specifies who may know what, when and in what detail. The code is strictly followed and constantly reinforced. Of their growing up, older *miminar* say: We listened to our Elders. We didn't question them. We wouldn't have dared. We waited to be told. Younger people demonstrate their respect for their Elders in their daily behaviour. They defer to their Elders and never address them by a first name without prefacing it with the appropriate kin term. Violating the respect system brings shame. In this way 'shame' reinforces the respect system. Shame is an aspect of your *miwi* [inner spirit] telling you things, letting you know what's right and wrong.

The stories of the Old People guide younger generations; the recounting brings sorrow and joy. The stories told here are ones that are owned; that highlight key aspects of caring for country; that emphasise how *ngatji* [totems], *ruwi* [country], *miwi* [inner spirit], weaving, bush tucker and medicine, care for children and care for country are interwoven in Ngarrindjeri identity. The women are concerned that the stories are kept alive. If we Elders die, then who passes on our culture, heritage, and stories? We need to look after our Elders with proper health care and housing and we need culturally appropriate ways of recording our stories of the past and present. We need to be telling those stories to young people, Aunty Margaret Dodd insisted. Telling stories helps me know where I fit into things and who I'm allowed to boss around and who can boss me around, said Aunty Eileen McHughes.

Younger women are aware that there is much to learn of Ngarrindjeri *ruwi* and culture from their Elders. They asked:

> What was it like for Mum and Dad when they were growing up?

Tell me the good and the bad?

How are our families related?

What bush tucker did you eat?

Here are three stories, told by Ngarrindjeri Elders, where they explain how they care for country.

Aunty Leila's story

The story of the funeral for Aunty Leila Rankine (1932–1993) is one that is told over and over. Aunty Maggie Jacobs (1920–2003), defender of her culture, story-teller and singer extraordinaire, speaks with respect and authority of the day her sister-in-law's ashes were scattered on the Coorong. Diane Bell: "I was working with the Ngarrindjeri women on the application to secure protection for their sacred places on *Kumarangk* (Hindmarsh Island) under the *Aboriginal and Torres Strait Islander Heritage Protection Act 1984* and they were explaining how *ngatji,* variously translated as 'friend, totem, countryman, protector', bring messages. I asked about *ngatji.* This is how Aunty Maggie told the story to Aunty Veronica Brodie, Leila's younger sister and me in 1996."

I'll tell you about *ngatji,* that totem. You know it was Leila's wish to come down and have one last look at all the countryside before she died. Well, the pelican is her *ngatji.* We brought Leila from Camp Coorong to Raukkan, and we had a bit of a service for Leila there. And when we went to go off, to leave Raukkan, and we came down to the ferry and, you know that little jetty at the Raukkan, there's always hundreds of pelicans, you know, they're always sitting there. *Una?* [Isn't it?] We started to come across but there was no pelicans. You see them in the water swimming, see them sitting, four of them sitting there. But that day there wasn't a pelican to be seen. We come along to the ferry and just before we pulled

Margaret 'Maggie' Jacobs (née Rankine) and her sister-in-law Leila Rankine (née Wilson)

Photograph: Margaret Jacob's personal collection, 1989

into the ferry, one pelican was sitting there, and he just looked in and we had the window open, and he, only one pelican, he just looked in to Leila and he went like this with his wings [Aunty Maggie folds her arms in and out across her chest]. You know, three or four times, and Veronica said to her sister, "Leila, look, he's saying goodbye to you." And that is exactly what he was doing, you know, he was saying goodbye. And Leila said, "Yeah."

Then, after she died, and we was having a service at Pelican Point, one pelican flew over, flew right over us, the group that was on the bank there. And Lizzie Rigney said, she said, "Oh look," she said, you know, "There's Aunty Leila, or old Granny Koomi [Leila and Veronica's mother] or somebody like that" because that's their *ngatji*. Anyway, after we finished the service and we got to the ranger boat to come down to Ngarlung and then all of a sudden there was another pelican and the pelican, you know, you usually see them in the dozens you know, but this time there was only one pelican, and this one pelican, other than the one that flew over us when we started off, there was one pelican, and when we got in the boat, the ranger boat, and the pelican flew low on the water, like this, right in front of us. [Aunty Maggie swoops with her arms.] It skimmed.

One pelican flew right in front of us, took us right over to where we were, but when we got off at Ngarlung and the women were singing the hymn, "God be with you." I carried Leila's ashes. Veronica and I went to walk up and we found it a bit hard, you know, because the sand was a bit heavy. And Tom [Trevorrow] said, "No, it's not the place; it's down further." There was only a few of us, those that were pretty close to Leila, and we started off again. And this one pelican, just the one pelican again, he was just almost touching the water and he flew right up, right to where we buried Leila, to where we put Leila's ashes, then he disappeared, see. All right, then that was all right. You know, Roslyn Milera, Leila's care person, she couldn't get over it. But we know what happens. *Una*, Veronica?

Ngori on the Coorong at the reburial ceremony for the Old People, September 20, 2006

Photograph: Vesper Tjukonai

That's the *ngatji*, you see. Our animals tell us everything.

By coming home to be buried, Aunty Leila made a statement about whose country it was and who should care for it. Future generations are being taught how to read the story, the significance of the single pelican leading the way; to remark on the spiritual associations with country; to watch the behaviour of *ngori* [pelican] and other *ngatji*; to see themselves as part of this world. When the Old People were returned to their country in 2006, and the pelicans led the way to the reburial site on the Coorong, Aunty Leila's story was recalled (see Chapter Three).

Leila Rankine returns to her *ruwi*: Scattering her ashes, Coorong, 1992

Kenny Sumner (great nephew), William and Keir Rankine (grandsons), George and Tom Trevorrow

Photograph: Margaret Jacob's personal collection

The only way Aunty Leila could be buried on her country was to have her ashes scattered. There are no official cemeteries in the hummocks on the Coorong. The site to which her kin were led by the pelican was a favourite Wilson [Veronica and Leila's father line] lookout, with full oversight of the spiritual breeding grounds of *ngatji*, and far enough back from the edge so that erosion would not disturb the place. Uncle George Trevorrow explained: She said this is where the meeting of the fresh and salt waters began. So that's why we brought Aunty Leila here. That was her wish and we carried it out. Aunty Leila is here.

Aunty Leila Rankine is remembered as a story-teller, poet, speech-maker and fighter for the rights of her people. Her poems tell of her feelings for her country and the importance of her spiritual ties to the area. In her poem, 'The Coorong' she wrote:

> Oh the spirit of the long ago
> And guardian of the past
> As I stand beside your waters
> My soul knows peace at last.
>
> *Leila Rankine (c1980)*

With the lack of water in the Murray-Darling system to flush the River, Lakes and Coorong and increased salinity – the Southern Coorong is now saltier than the Dead Sea – the *ngori* [pelican] breeding grounds are shrinking. This *ngatji* is no longer thriving in its own *ruwi*. The stress on the *ngatji* echoes the stressed *ruwi* and stressed people.

Aunty Ellen's story

Aunty Ellen Trevorrow is a cultural weaver. It's a meditation, she says. Her work has been exhibited at home and abroad. The getting of the rushes (*Cyperus gymnocaulos*), the preparation, the working, and the teaching are core activities that connect Aunty Ellen to her *ruwi*. Diane: "At various times over the last decade Aunty Ellen has told me her story of growing up on the River, of moving to the Coorong, and has shared her feelings about the country. She worries about the well-being of the land. She grieves the damage done to her country." When I went across to *Kumarangk* [Hindmarsh Island] for the first time, Aunty Ellen explains, I was with my Elders and I felt it in my tummy, all stirred up, and I cried. And that's when I believed what my Elders were saying about the island being sacred women's business. When I went home that night and told Tom, he said that it was my *miwi* speaking to me, so it's true.

Here is Aunty Ellen Trevorrow's story.

I was born at Raukkan, Point McLeay, and then I was taken with my grandmother to live at *Murrunggung* [Brinkley], that's just this side of Wellington, so we were at the tail end of the River. I grew up there til the age of eleven. Everything was so plentiful. It was a beautiful area and it still is today but then my grandmother would take us fishing. We'd fish, up and down. She'd spin. We'd fish for some nice *pondi* [Murray Cod] and row them up to Wellington and sell them. We'd go down to where Lake Alexandrina and the River meet, to where we call 'Leeches'. My grandmother would fish there and she would also go up and collect the *thukabi ngartheri* [turtle eggs] to take back. We experienced a lot of the Lake there and the River and where the River and Lake meet. That was my lifestyle with my grandmothers, right up to the age of eleven. It was a beautiful area to us but when I go back up around the River area now, the River is going in a bad way. The fish, the birds, it's all in a bad way.

Basket weaving was all around me as a child, but it wasn't my mother or grandmother who taught me. They said I needed to have an education, a white education. The welfare department would take children away if they didn't go to school. So I missed out on a lot as a child, but in my late forties my mother started to pass on important cultural information to me because we were running Camp Coorong. I was taught weaving by Aunty Dorrie Kartinyeri [née Gollan], around 1980 at a workshop that was arranged by the South Australian Museum with Steve Hemming and Aunty Dorrie. She was an Elder and I always thanked her for teaching me weaving. I enjoyed weaving, because I reminisced on my life, my childhood and my grandmother, my family and the basket weaving. From then on, I was teaching the basket weaving and my first class was a Year Nine at Meningie. I've been teaching ever since and working towards exhibitions.

The rushes like fresh water and a lot of considerate farmers leave them so we have supplies. I move around and just thin out the good places. I'm finding it very hard down our end close to the Coorong because there was a lot there, but the salt water table is taking over. We need fresh water. Sometimes along the roadside, because it's not on the farmer's property, but just where the water runs off the road, the rushes are growing very nice, and you'll see someone picking them. But I move around in a cycle. I pick and move and let the other lot grow. They grow very quick. Later I can return when the young ones have come up again. You can see where I've been.

Ellen Trevorrow collecting rushes, Strathalbyn, April 2006

Photograph: Vesper Tjukonai

My Nanna Brown made baskets to sell or to make trade for some clothing or something for us. After the age of eleven, I moved to Bonney Reserve with my mum. I did my schooling at Meningie and straight from school I went into a family with my husband Tom Trevorrow. He was working for a fisherman at the time and we would eat a lot of fish. My life is based from *Murrunggung* to Meningie and that's where I still am today, here with my family, weaving. It's cultural weaving because I use the same rushes that my Old People used – it's the three-pronged

Ellen Trevorrow weaving at the end of a long day, Camp Coorong, June 22, 2007

Photograph: Diane Bell

type of fresh water rushes – there's a lot of different types of rushes, but this is one that was used because it lasts a long time. Weaving is not just something I do to make money. I don't sell a lot. I work towards exhibitions. I love teaching. I love sharing the basket weaving.

Aunty Ellen Trevorrow, eldest daughter of Mrs Daisy Rankine, is named after Nanna Ellen Brown, the daughter of Margaret 'Pinkie' Mack whose stories and songs were recorded by anthropologists Ronald and Catherine Berndt in the early 1940s (Berndt C. 1994a; Berndt *et al* 1993). Pinkie Mack's mother, Louisa Karpany could remember the early white explorers who came into her country. Aunty Ellen makes these connections for the next generation: Every time we go past Murrunggung, I tell the same story. Luke gets sick of it. Una? But if there is a new face in the car, I tell it again. I share with the nieces and nephews. "This is where Nanna collected rushes," I tell them. "It's an honour to pick rushes where Nanna picked them."

Ngarrindjeri weaving is visible in the early European record of settlement in South Australia. In 1833, explorer Charles Sturt (1833:155) described the circular mats on which women sat. In the 1840s, artist George French Angas (1844, 1847) drew them. In the 1870s, Taplin (1873:43) wrote of women's weaving and mentioned they had mats to sell. In a 1915 photograph of 'Queen' Louisa Karpany, there are baskets of the design now made by her great, great granddaughter Aunty Ellen Trevorrow. In a 1927 newspaper article about Granny Ethel Wympie Watson, we read of how the "gift of a beautifully made basket made in green and red rushes indicated that this primitive [sic] art is still being practiced" and of how the reporter talked with Granny Ethel Wympie Watson about the old times "of corroborees we had both witnessed and of the subsequent lavish suppers provided by my mother. 'Those were the days,' said Ethel furtively wiping away a tear..." (E.S.A. 1927). Baskets such as these are on display at Camp Coorong and Ngarrindjeri *miminar* continue to demonstrate their skills and knowledge with their weaving.

Sister Basket made by Ethel Wympie Watson, 1939

Photograph: M. Kluvanek, N.B.Tindale Collection A 15951, South Australian Museum, Anthropology Archives

'Queen' Louisa Karpany and companion, c. 1915
Photograph: M. Angas collection, South Australian Museum, Anthropology Archives

Margaret 'Pinkie' Mack, Brinkley, c. 1943
Photograph: R.M. Berndt Collection, South Australian Museum, Anthropology Archive

Weaving through the ages

Laura Isobelle Kartinyeri (née Sumner), Murray Bridge, c.1980s (Sister of Ellen Brown)
Photograph: Doreen Kartinyeri's personal collection

Seven Generations of Weaving Women

Louisa Karpany 1821–1921
Margaret 'Pinkie' Mack 1858-1954
Ellen Brown 1905-1979,
    sister of Laura Kartinyeri 1906-1995
Daisy Rankine 1936
Ellen Trevorrow 1955
Tanya Trevorrow 1978
Ellen Wilson 1996

Ellen Trevorrow, Daisy Rankine, Ellen 'Ellie' Wilson, Tanya Trevorrow
Photograph: Ellen Trevorrow's personal collection, 1996

9

Aunty Ellen Trevorrow: The thing is now, is today, I'm a weaver. The rushes are a part of our culture that the land provides for us. The land is already salting up, and pesticides are ruining our rushes. We have to travel a long way today to collect our freshwater rushes for weaving. To go and collect the rushes where my grandmother collected her rushes, there's nothing there. There isn't any. It's a really big change in our environment and it's very important to look after it. We've got to look after it, especially for our children. If you look at us now, what are we leaving behind for our children? What are we leaving behind?

The River is in a bad way. Now there's talk about a weir down the end, there past Wellington at Pomanda Island. What's our direction? It's very important for us to look after what we've got because we're leaving something behind. Like I said with the rushes, I'm looking all the time, I'm coming right over to Strathalbyn, to collect rushes. That's saying enough just for the rushes, let alone the fish and the birds we caught around our area. There were nice size fishes.

When I first moved to the Coorong, I thought, "Hey, look at this!" The

The entrance to Camp Coorong, May 3, 2005
Photograph: Vesper Tjukonai

environment was so good because where I had been living, the land was cleared. And then to go down to the Coorong, down at Bonney Reserve, there was lots of everything. There was a big difference, but now there are big changes. What I mean, I moved here when I was eleven, I spent my life there on the River, it was beautiful, there was lots of everything. On the Coorong, there was lots of everything, but what do we have now?

What is our direction?

Where are we going?

What are we leaving behind?

There's our young ones, our children and their children.

We're all of an age. I'm talking of ages about what I've experienced. We have to put things right for our young ones. It's most important. I feel really bad when I hear us arguing about one bit of water. What about looking after the whole river?

Uncle Tom and Aunty Ellen Trevorrow bring their knowledge of their country and their concerns to their work at Camp Coorong (Hemming

1993). They say: We teach our Ngarrindjeri basket-weaving techniques. We tell of our stories relating to the land, waters, trees, plants, birds and animals – people call them our Dreaming stories. They are our way of life, our survival teaching stories.

Aunty Eileen's story

Aunty Eileen McHughes had many opportunities for hearing stories from her Elders and learning about the country first hand while living with her extended family at the Three Mile Camp at Tailem Bend and holidaying at the One Mile Camp at Meningie. The eldest of eight siblings, Aunty Eileen traces her family line through her father to Old Kropinyeri who died in 1875; through her mother's father's line to Old Gollan (1817–77); and through her mother's mother's line to Adeline Sumner (1890–1932) born on the Coorong. These are important Ngarrindjeri lineages. Her mother died when the youngest child was only five and Eileen became the one who told the stories. This was before television, Eileen's younger sister, Vicki Hartman, says, Eileen shared with us. We'd sit around *yunnan*. She'd tell us about the *mulyawongk* hole at Tailem Bend and not to swim until the dandelions had died off – otherwise you'd get sick and turn yellow.

Here Aunty Eileen McHughes tells of the *mingka* bird, the messenger of death. It is a story that many Ngarrindjeri know, but Aunty Eileen is one of the few people who has seen the bird.

Down at the One Mile Camp at Meningie, I guess I was about eleven or twelve. I remember Aunty Marj Koolmatrie and Bill, Aunty Tingie and Nulla [Richards], Jean Gollan [Neville Gollan's mother], Granny Rosie from Kingston way, Aunty Pud and Uncle Mervyn, Uncle [George] Walker and his wife, George Johnston and Aunty Thora Lampard [mother of George and Tom Trevorrow] were all there. It was getting towards evening and all us kids, we were playing outside, running through the bushes and scaring each

Sisters Vicki Hartman and Eileen McHughes, and Eileen's daughter Georgie Trevorrow, Camp Coorong, June 23, 2007

Photograph: Diane Bell

other, when we heard this noise. We knew it was a bird, but we didn't know what kind of bird it was. The Old People just gathered us up and popped us inside. They even covered the windows up. It was a *mingka* bird. The next day we knew something had happened because they had begun crying, and it wasn't crying like we cry. It was wailing and it went on all day and half the next.

Then, when I was about twelve, it was when we had moved up to Tailem Bend, and I was going down to the River for a swim. I walked past the trees going down and something caught my eye. I felt a little bit scared but I was nosey and wanted to know. I went back and parted the leaves and there was this little bird. The face looked almost human, it had actual, real eyelashes. People really think I'm weird now [in telling the story]. Dad came looking for me. When we walked back up the cliff, I told Dad about the bird and showed him. He said it was a *mingka* bird. Previously, I thought the *mingka* bird was a mopoke, but it's not. It's different. It's a grey bird. The one I saw was about the size of a Murray Magpie. When I close my eyes I can still see it. When you go up to a bird it usually flies away. I know not many people have seen it but I'm sure about what I saw.

They told me when it cries like a baby, a baby dies. When it cries like a woman, a woman dies, and when it is a deeper sort of cry is when a man dies.

Diane: "We were taking a break from the workshop, sitting outside in the weak winter sun and Aunty Eileen began talking about her *ngatji*." The tiger snake is Aunty Eileen and Aunty Vicki's *ngatji* on their father's side. They tell stories of a tiger snake, attracted by the music from the vibrations of an old wind up player, coming up from the River. It was at the Three Mile Camp. We had a big tarp on the ground and the women were washing and yarning. The snake came right up to the tub. Eileen has many stories about snakes. Grandfather Mike told us about one of his uncles putting a rag in a snake's mouth, pulling out the fangs and stitching up the lips. Then there was a brown snake that chased one of the grandchildren at Camp Coorong. Just over there, says Aunty Eileen pointing beyond where we are sitting. And there are stories of putting a snake under your shirt to keep it warm. Aunty Eileen explains: I was taught the tiger snake was my *ngatji* on my father's side and the huntsman spider is our *ngatji* on our mother's side. We were taught to have respect, not to harm our *ngatji*.

The Ngarrindjeri *miminar*'s stories provide a framework for thinking about the future. This is what they had to say:

Our *ngatji* need protection. We can't just get up and move. This is our place. There are special places where we can show our kids Ngarrindjeri *ruwi*

and keep our culture alive, teach them about bush tucker and bush
medicine. There are places with long uninterrupted histories of
Ngarrindjeri care, places where we can fish on the Coorong, the ocean.
Places like Bonney Reserve, *Warnung* (Hack's Point), Raukkan. Places
where we collect rushes.

We'd like to visit the Three Mile Camp at Tailem Bend, the One Mile Camp
at Meningie and tell younger ones about what life was like there.

It is good to visit the Granites, the 42 Mile, Boundary Bluff, but
transportation can be a problem.

Aunty Eileen recalls being taken on the back of a truck from Tailem Bend
to the Lakes to fish. Some would be cooked and eaten there and some would
be taken home. The women are sad that today they can't get to some of
their places. In some places, developments
and subdivisions along the River and Lakes
have restricted Ngarrindjeri access to favourite
camping sites and resources.

We used to go to Leeches for turtle eggs.

Where can we go to gather bush tucker?

Where can we gather pelican feathers to
make feather flowers?

Where can we gather swan eggs?

We want access to our traditional food, to
the material resources we need for events
like for NAIDOC [National Aboriginal and
Islander Day Observance Committee) Day and
cultural events.

Karla bush scones, May 2005

Photograph: Vesper Tjukonai

Aunty Hilda Day, Aunty Noreen Kartinyeri, Katie Reid,
Georgina Trevorrow and Dorothy Kartinyeri listed the
bush tucker they wanted to grow and collect and learn
about. We need land where we can grow rushes, places
where we can revegetate, where we could grow *nganangi*,
pig face [*Carpobrotus rossii*]. You can eat the fruit, it's juicy,
and the leaves are good medicine for mosquito bites. There
is *Kundawi* [*Billardiera sp*], a long thin like capsule, it's a sweet
fruit; *munthari* [*Kunzea pomifera*], a sweet apple berry; *karla*
[*Acacia longifolia*], the seeds are gathered, crushed and
can be eaten in a damper; *mulbukuti*, a sweet round fruit,

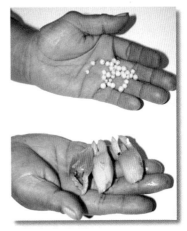

Ngarrindjeri *miminar*'s hands with
nganingi and *kalathumi*,
January 2008

Photograph: Vesper Tjukonai

Ellie Wilson and Rachel Day collect *munthari*, May 2005

Photograph: Anne McMahon

Rachel Day and Hank Trevorrow, May 2005

Photograph: Anne McMahon

Tayla-Jayde Wilson, Innes 'Ninny' Rigney, Gail Brennan, Macey-Lee Wilson at Bonney Reserve where they had collected bush foods, October, 2007

Photograph: Vesper Tjukonai

it grows on the underneath of a spiky plant; *yalkuri*, Old man's beard [*Clematis microphylla*]; *peeintuk* [*Dianella sp*] good for sore throats; *kalathumi* [*Leucopogon parviflorus*] a coastal heath. We need clean water. We need to care for water ways – no water, no food.

Aunty Ellen and her granddaughter, Ellie Wilson, talk about times they have been collecting cockles. Ellen: It was February this year [2007]. We crossed the Coorong, near Hack's Point, that's the narrowest part, and walked to the ocean side where we got cockles. We returned at Parnka Point and Tom met us in the car. Tanya led the way across the Coorong. She's in front, guiding us across, and Hank is leading the group through the water. I was waiting on the shore with the others. We had a girl who couldn't do the walk and Tanya came back and helped us across. Ellie talks about dancing for cockles to bring them up and demonstrates by swirling. When asked where she learned the cockle dance, Ellie says, With my family. Aunty Ellen smiles, They're always along side us. I've got photos of Luke and Joe doing the same thing.

The Ngarrindjeri *miminar* wanted to make sure their knowledge was kept alive. This is what Aunty Thelma Smart, Aunty Helen Jackson and Donna Kartinyeri said: We want videos, booklets, posters about our country, ones that make us proud, show what we have been doing. We want our

Crossing the Coorong near Hack's Point, February 10, 2007

Photograph: Barry Crush

Elders to go into schools and camps and so on to tell our stories. We want this sharing and caring. Aunty Rita Lindsay, Aunty Ellen Trevorrow, Aunty Alice Abdulla and Aunty Margaret Dodd added: We want our young people to be educated so they can be part of managing our lands and waters, so they will have employment, so land and waters will be cared for according to Ngarrindjeri laws, for future generations. Looking ahead, the women saw these paths to employment for future generations as being part of creating a secure world, one in which they had independence and were not reliant on governments. Economic development that has caring for country as a goal is a priority.

Cockles, June 2006

Photograph: Anne McMahon

Ellie Wilson doing the 'Cockle Dance', Southern Ocean, across the Coorong from Parnka Point, June 2006

Photograph: Anne McMahon

The *Kumarangk* story

The dedication of Ngarrindjeri *miminar* to caring for country came to national attention with the struggle to protect sacred places in the *Kumarangk* (Hindmarsh Island), Goolwa, and Murray Mouth area. Telling the story is painful.[6] The legal history is tortuous. The ethnographic 'facts' contested. The media reporting uneven. The reality for the Ngarrindjeri is that their personal lives have become public property and the knowledge of their Old People has been challenged and treated with disrespect. Healing is needed but it will take time and resolve along the lines of the February 13, 2008 'Apology to Australia's Indigenous People' by Prime Minister Kevin Rudd (2008) to write "this new page in the history of our great continent."

Perhaps, at some future date, it may be possible to write this 'new page' without reference to the various legal proceedings that probed the authenticity of the claim by the Ngarrindjeri women who brought two applications under the *Aboriginal and Torres Strait Islander Heritage Protection Act, 1984*. Perhaps not. Some legal narratives have wider circulation than others.[7] Here is an outline of key moments in matters Hindmarsh.[8]

1994: The first Heritage application. The proposal to build a bridge from the mainland at Goolwa across the channel to *Kumarangk* in order to service a marina on the island was opposed by a number of groups (environmentalists, local residents, unionists). However, it was the Ngarrindjeri women, who believed that the building of the bridge across those waters would desecrate their sacred places, and the men who were supporting them, who took decisive legal action and fought until they exhausted all legal remedies available to them. A 25 year ban, the maximum possible under the Heritage Act, was placed on development of the site. The ban was short lived. It was set aside on technical grounds: Robert Tickner, then Minister of Aboriginal Affairs had not read all the documents, but rather, had respected the restrictions placed on two appendices to the Report of Cheryl Saunders (1994). Aunty Doreen Kartinyeri had reluctantly agreed to write down part of the sacred story she knew and have it placed in a sealed envelope labelled "TO BE READ BY WOMEN ONLY".

1995: The Royal Commission. The restriction was not honoured for long. The so-called 'secret envelopes' were brandished in Federal Parliament in March 1995 by Ian McLachlan, then Minister for the Environment and Member for Barker, a district that takes in Goolwa and Hindmarsh Island (see

Fergie 1994; 1996). A group of Ngarrindjeri women spoke out saying they did not know the story about 'women's business' (Wilson 1998). The Royal Commission heard from these women but Aunty Dodo, as the late Doreen Kartinyeri is fondly known, refused to appear before the Royal Commission and in her absence, she and the other applicants were found to have fabricated beliefs to thwart development on *Kumarangk* (Stevens 1995).

At the time, Aunty Ellen Trevorrow said I believe in my Elders and I love them for what they're doing and I'm sorry that all of this has happened this way for my Elders because it's drained us all.

1996: The second Heritage application. As soon as the findings of the Royal Commission were known, a second application was lodged but the Mathews Report (1996) was set aside in mid-1996 when the High Court ruled that the appointment by the Commonwealth government of Justice Jane Mathews, a Federal Court judge, as the person to report on the Heritage application was ineffective.[9]

Victor Wilson of Murray Bridge paid tribute to the women in his 1996 song that was first sung at Amelia Park, Goolwa, the site of many protests and the site of the Ngarrindjeri Embassy.

> My clan woman sister,
> We owe so much to you,
> You're our mother, our aunty, our grandmother too,
> You're a stateswoman, freedom fighter, defender of our land.
> My clan woman sister, we stand in awe of you.

1997–8: *Hindmarsh Island Bridge Act 1997*. This piece of Commonwealth legislation said that sacred sites could be protected anywhere but on Hindmarsh Island. The Ngarrindjeri High Court challenge to this legislation brought in the High Court by Doreen Kartinyeri and Neville Gollan failed because the court held that the government could pass laws and the government could amend laws.[10] From this perspective, the new law was not discriminatory, simply an amendment of an existing law. The outcome for the Ngarrindjeri applicants was that Australian law had failed to protect places sacred to women. The Ngarrindjeri applicants had not had their day in court.

1997–2001: The Compensation Case.[11] Federal Court Judge von Doussa heard from all parties to the dispute: those who knew the story and believed that *Kumarangk* was sacred to women; those who contested the existence and

Hindmarsh Island Bridge Act, 1997, The High Court, Canberra, February 5, 1998
Back row: Eunice Aston, Diane Bell, Doreen Kartinyeri, Veronica Brodie, Hazel Wilson
Front row: Dorothy Shaw, Margaret Jacobs, Grace Sumner, Cherie Watkins
Photograph: Cherie Watkins' personal collection

content of the knowledge; anthropologists, historians and museum men; a federal Minister and a law professor. There was rigorous cross-examination. The hearings ran from December 1999 to March 2001, and produced thousands of pages of transcript and hundreds of exhibits.

Judge von Doussa found Doreen Kartinyeri to be a credible witness: "I am not prepared to find that her evidence about the circumstances in which she received the restricted women's knowledge from Aunty Rosie, and about the knowledge itself, is a lie" (von Doussa 2001:para 310). Aunty Dodo used to say, What was my intent? Why would I have lied about my culture? No-one ever asked me that. It seems that it is easier to construct the women as liars than to come to terms with their passionate commitment to care for their country.

How to explain the finding of fabrication in 1995? In his 'Reasons for Decision' delivered on August 21, 2001, von Doussa (para 12) wrote:

> The evidence received by the Court on this topic is significantly different to that which was before the Royal Commission. Upon the evidence

> before this Court I am not satisfied that the restricted women's knowledge
> was fabricated or that it was not part of genuine Aboriginal tradition.

This vindication of the Ngarrindjeri offered some comfort to those who had been labelled liars but came too late to stop the bridge. It was built and opened to traffic on March 4, 2001. As foretold, women became ill.

In the course of the Royal Commission, the term 'secret women's business' became the brunt of sexist, racist and deeply offensive jokes. The Ngarrindjeri fight for their *ruwi*,[12] their country, became an inquiry into women's *ruwar*, their bodies. The relationship between body and land is marked in the language – *ruwar* is the plural of *ruwi* – and is evident in Ngarrindjeri beliefs and practices about their *ngatji* as their friend, country-man and totem. As we heard in Aunty Maggie's story of the scattering of Aunty Leila's ashes, *ngori* [pelican] led the way. Her *ngatji* brings her *ruwar* home to her *ruwi* on the Coorong.

Ngarrindjeri Embassy, *Pulgi, Kumarangk*, 2000

Rita Lindsay, Audrey Lindsay, Michael Lindsay, Rita Lindsay Jr, Marian Thompson, Paul Norvill and niece, Dave Sjoberg

Photograph: Vesper Tjukonai

A number of women at the forefront of the struggle have passed away. I really miss her, Aunty Ellen said at Aunty Veronica's funeral on May 11, 2007. She was such a support for us all. Aunty Veronica was a respected Elder, a trailblazer in the formation of many community initiatives and organisations. In her book, *My Side of the Bridge*, Aunty Veronica wrote: It's been a long-drawn-out process and a lot of hurts have been brought out with it, and a healing process needs to start now among the women

Michele Gollan and Natasha Sumner, smoking ceremony, Amelia Park, September 18, 1999

Photograph: Vesper Tjukonai

Veronica Brodie and Margaret Jacobs, Federal Court, Adelaide, August 21, 2001

Judge John von Doussa rejects the claim that the Ngarrindjeri women who fought against the building of the bridge to Hindmarsh Island were fabricators. "I knowed I was no liar," Aunty Maggie announced as she left the court.

Photograph: Diane Bell

(Brodie 2007:143). For her, the Old People are still on the island and the spirits still walk the island. You cannot take away the fact that the Ngarrindjeri women's business did take place on Hindmarsh Island (*ibid*.:144).

Now there is a generation of young women who have come to maturity during and since the struggle to protect Ngarrindjeri places on *Kumarangk*. Any discussion that takes up the issue of the safety and integrity of women's bodies is likely to evoke bitter memories of the struggle to protect their sacred places on *Kumarangk*. The stories are being kept alive. The NRA is the body with whom all future developers will have to deal. The tragedy of *Kumarangk* must never be repeated.

A story of practical reconciliation

In September 2002, an excavation that was part of the Goolwa wharf redevelopment project desecrated the burial site of a Ngarrindjeri mother and child (Hemming and Trevorrow 2005). Ngarrindjeri knew their Old People had been buried on the site. They had said so during the struggle to protect *Kumarangk*. The site was listed by the South Australian Department of Aboriginal Affairs and Reconciliation. But the approach of members of the Alexandrina Council had been that the site was part of the colonial history of the River. Goolwa was a river port to be redeveloped: this was where the wooden boats festival was celebrated. In their view, Ngarrindjeri interests had been washed away. It seemed that little had changed since the bridge – only metres away from the redevelopment – had been built. The Ngarrindjeri could have taken legal action against the Council. Instead, after a month of intense negotiations, they chose to lead by example; to bring members of the Alexandrina Council into their world of caring for country, stories, and Old People by negotiating an agreement.

The *Kungun Ngarrindjeri Yunnan* (Listen to Ngarrindjeri Talking) agreement signed on October 8, 2002 by the Alexandrina Council and the Ngarrindjeri was a step towards rebuilding trust.

Kungun Ngarrindjeri Yunnan Agreement:

1. **Apology**

   The Council will make a public apology to the Ngarrindjeri as expressed in Schedule 1 of this Agreement.

2. **Acknowledgment**

   2.1 The Council acknowledges that the Ngarrindjeri are the Traditional Owners of the Coorong area and that according to their traditions, customs and spiritual beliefs its lands and waters remain their traditional country.

   2.2 The Council also acknowledges and respects the rights, interests and obligations of Ngarrindjeri to speak and care for their traditional country, lands and waters as an identifiable group of people in accordance with their laws, customs, beliefs and traditions.

   2.3 Each Party has authority to enter into this Agreement and to make the acknowledgements and commitments referred to herein.

   2.4 The Parties acknowledge the Background as true and correct.

3. **Commitment**

   3.1 The Parties commit to together seek ways to uphold Ngarrindjeri rights and to advance Ngarrindjeri interests and cultural economy when decisions are being made about their traditional country, lands and waters.

   3.2 The Parties commit to work together to advance harmonious community relations.

   3.3 The Parties commit to develop greater community understanding of Ngarrindjeri traditions, culture, laws and spiritual beliefs in the Council area.

   3.4 The Parties commit to work together to determine, and to advance the community recognition of, a framework agreement for the protection of Aboriginal sites, objects and remains in relation to the Council area.

   3.5 The Parties commit to the formulation of a model or models of best practice for consultation in relation to development assessment within the meaning of the *Development Act 1993* (SA) to occur in the Council area, which reflects the rights, interests and obligations of the Ngarrindjeri.

   3.6 The Parties will establish a joint committee comprising equal numbers of Ngarrindjeri and Council representatives to develop a strategy for the implementation of the commitments expressed herein, whose name will be determined by the committee.

   3.7 This Clause 3 is made as an act of good faith and is not intended to affect the legal rights, powers, obligations or interests of either Party.

In the letter of apology the Alexandrina Council wrote:

> To the Ngarrindjeri people, the traditional owners of the land and waters within the region, the Alexandrina Council expresses sorrow and sincere regret for the suffering and injustice that you have experienced since colonisation and we share with you our feelings of shame and sorrow at the mistreatment your people have suffered...

> We are shamed to acknowledge that there is still racism within our communities. We accept that our words must match our actions and we pledge to you that we will work to remove racism and ignorance... (see Appendix One for the full text).

By saying sorry for the wrong, acknowledging the Ngarrindjeri as the traditional owners of the land and showing respect for their culture, the Alexandrina Council has engaged in what the Ngarrindjeri leadership terms an act of 'practical reconciliation'. But the story does not end there.

A burying of past differences, Goolwa Wharf, October 17, 2002

Seated in centre: Margaret Jacobs, Veronica Brodie. Kneeling: Corina Trevorrow and Kyra Rankine

Standing: Ellie Wilson, Justin Sumner, Neville Gollan, Dorothy Turnbull (with walking stick), Sandra Saunders, Doreen Kartinyeri, Belinda Stillisano, Glenys Wilson, Cherie Watkins, Marshall Carter, Major Sumner (with boomerangs), Gary Paynter, Jordan Sumner

Photo courtesy of *The Times*, Victor Harbor, South Australia

The Old People whose grave had been desecrated had to be laid to rest according to Ngarrindjeri law. On October 17, 2002, with proper ceremony and support of the local council and state government, the Ngarrindjeri reburied the woman and child. In so doing, Ngarrindjeri Old People became part of the renegotiated landscape of a major rural town (Hemming and Trevorrow 2005:255).

Future stories

At the first workshop at Camp Coorong on June 24 2007, it was agreed that Women need a healthy environment. When the discussion turned to governance issues (see Chapter Four), the women saw benefits flowing from protocols like *Kungun Ngarrindjeri Yunnan* agreement. They looked forward to being able to read their words and *Yarluwar-Ruwe Plan* (Ngarrindjeri Tendi *et al* 2006) together. They thought that by establishing a Caring for Country Centre as part of, or in collaboration with, existing Ngarrindjeri organisations we could all enjoy a healthy environment.

One way forward is through the implementation of the *Yarluwar-Ruwe Plan* (Sea-Country Plan) of the Ngarrindjeri Nation (Ngarrindjeri Tendi *et al* 2006:1).

> Our goals are:
> - For our people, children and descendants to be healthy and to enjoy our healthy lands and waters.
> - To see our lands and waters healthy and spiritually alive.
> - For all our people to benefit from our equity in our lands and waters.
> - To see our closest friends – our *Ngartjis* – healthy and spiritually alive.
> - For our people to continue to occupy and benefit from our lands and waters.
> - To see all people respecting our laws and living in harmony with our lands and waters.

The Caring for Country Centre, as proposed in the Plan (*ibid.*:33) would be a place where government agencies, industry and non-government organisations could negotiate and work with Ngarrindjeri on plans concerning the protection and management of Ngarrindjeri *ruwi*, under the direction of Ngarrindjeri people. As the Caring for Country Centre and projects related to caring for country develop, it will be important that women are involved at all stages.

Ngarrindjeri *miminar*'s stories offer insights concerning their priorities and cautions regarding how best to proceed. They need access to their places to gather materials, to be at peace in the home of their forebears, to be able to teach their children and grannies [grandchildren]. They need to be able to share the stories of their places under conditions of their own making. They have a contribution to make on issues such as the increased salinity of the waterways and its impact on their *ngatji*, many of which are now endangered or displaced. It is, as Aunty Ellen teaches the next generation, an honour to pick rushes where Nanna picked them. We were, Aunty Eileen emphasises, taught to have respect, not to harm our *ngatji*.

Caring for Stories

Chapter 2

> Stitch by stitch,
> Circle by circle,
> Weaving is like the creation of life,
> All things are connected.
>
> *Aunty Ellen Trevorrow (Ngarrindjeri Tendi et al 2006:51)*

> Our Lands, Our Waters, Our People, All living things are connected.
> We implore people to respect our *Ruwe* (Country)
> as it was created by *Kaldowinyeri* (the Creation).
>
> *(Ngarrindjeri Tendi et al 2006:5)*

Stories of connection

Creation stories, passed from generation to generation, weave the world of Ngarrindjeri Land, Waters and People. All things are connected. *Ngurunderi*, creator of the River Murray, Lakes Alexandrina and Albert, the Coorong, the Hummocks, of Ngarrindjeri lands, waters, fish and resources, gave his people stories by which they could live and in which they could find meaning. He laid out the Law of Land. The story of *Muntjinggar* [Seven Sisters, Pleiades Constellation] tells of the trials and tribulations of young women in their passage to womanhood. The stories of the Seven Sisters and *Ngurunderi* intertwine at Goolwa. Women's stories and men's stories are part of the *Kaldowinyeri*. The story of the creation of different dialects of Ngarrindjeri from the body of *Wururi*, a female huntsman spider, is a powerful metaphor for the unity of the Ngarrindjeri Nation. All things are connected.

Creation stories are not told lightly. People earn the right to be told a story and not everyone knows everything. Stories are passed down according to considerations of place in family, aptitude and disposition. Stories are layered. Cautionary tales are told to children to keep them safe. The deeper meanings of stories will only be revealed when the Elders deem the time to be right. Some meanings are available to women, some to men. Stories are constantly vivified by being in country: *ngatji* bring messages, *miwi* can bring you home.

The story of *Ngurunderi*

The *Ngurunderi* story reaches across Ngarrindjeri *ruwi*. The story, as told here, was negotiated with senior members of the Ngarrindjeri Nation. It draws on the text in the *Yarluwar-Ruwe Plan* (Ngarrindjeri Tendi *et al* 2006:8), the text in the 1989 *Ngurunderi* exhibit, originally on display in the South Australian Museum and now on permanent display at the Ngarrindjeri Museum at Camp Coorong (Hemming *et al* 1989) and conversations in 2007 with the Ngarrindjeri Lands and Progress Association.[13]

A long, long time ago *Ngurunderi*, our Spiritual Ancestor, travelled down the River Murray in a bark canoe in search of his two wives who had run away from him. At that time the River was only a small stream below the junction with the Darling River. A giant Murray Cod, *Pondi*, swam ahead of *Ngurunderi*. *Pondi* had nowhere to go, so he went ploughing and crashing through the land. His huge body and tail created the mighty River Murray. Near Murray Bridge *Ngurunderi* threw a spear, but it missed and was changed into *Lentelin* (Long Island). At *Tagalung* (Tailem Bend) he threw another spear. The giant fish surged ahead and created a long straight stretch in the River. When *Nepeli* and *Ngurunderi* caught *Pondi*, at the place where the fresh and salt water meet, they cut him up into many pieces and made the fresh and salt water fish for the Ngarrindjeri people. To the last piece *Ngurunderi* said, "You keep being a *Pondi*."

Meanwhile, *Ngurunderi's* two wives, the sisters of *Nepeli*, had made camp. On their camp fire they were cooking *thurkeri* (bony bream), a fish forbidden to Ngarrindjeri *miminar*. *Ngurunderi* smelt the fish cooking and knew his wives were close. He abandoned his camp and came after them. His huts became two hills and his bark canoe became the Milky Way. Hearing *Ngurunderi* coming, his two wives just had time to build a raft of reeds and grass trees and to escape across

Lake Albert. On the other side, their raft turned back into reeds and grass trees. The women hurried south.

Ngurunderi followed his wives as far south as Kingston. Here he met the great sorcerer, *Purumpari*. The two men fought, using weapons and magic powers, until *Ngurunderi* won. He burned *Purumpari's* body in a huge fire, symbolised by granite boulders today, and turned north along the Coorong Beach. Here he camped several times, digging soaks in the sand for fresh water and fishing in the Coorong lagoon. *Ngurunderi* made his way across the Murray Mouth and along Encounter Bay towards Victor Harbor. He made a fishing ground near Middleton by throwing a huge tree into the sea to make a seaweed bed. Here he hunted a seal, its dying gasps can still be heard among the rocks. At Port Elliot he camped and fished again, without seeing a sign of his wives. He became angry and threw his spears into the sea at Victor Harbor, creating the islands there. Finally, after resting in a giant granite shade-shelter on *Kaike* (Granite Island), *Ngurunderi* heard his wives laughing and playing in the water near King's Beach. He hurled his club to the ground, creating *Longkuwar* (the Bluff) and strode after them.

His wives fled along the beach in terror until they reached Cape Jervis. At this time Kangaroo Island was still connected to the mainland, and the two wives began to hurry across to it. *Ngurunderi* had arrived at Cape Jervis, and seeing his wives still fleeing from him, he called out in the voice of thunder for the waters to rise. The women were swept from their path by huge waters and soon drowned. They became the rocky Page Islands.

Ngurunderi knew that it was time to leave this world and to enter the spirit world. He crossed to Kangaroo Island and travelled to the western end. After first throwing his spears into the sea, he dived in, before rising to become a bright star in the Milky Way.

As noted in *Yarluwar-Ruwe Plan* (Ngarrindjeri Tendi *et al* 2006:13), the waters of the seas, the waters of the *Kurangk* [Coorong], the waters of the rivers and the lakes are all spiritual waters. The Creation ancestors taught us how to respect and understand the connections between the lands, waters and the sky. The place where the fresh and salt waters mix is a place of creation where our *Ngartjis* [ngatji] breed. Our women fought to protect these spiritual waters from desecration by building a bridge to *Kumarangk* [Hindmarsh Island]. Any future plans affecting these waters must respect our cultural traditions and beliefs. We implore non-Indigenous people to respect the *Yarluwar-Ruwe* as it was created in the *Kaldowinyeri* [the Creation].

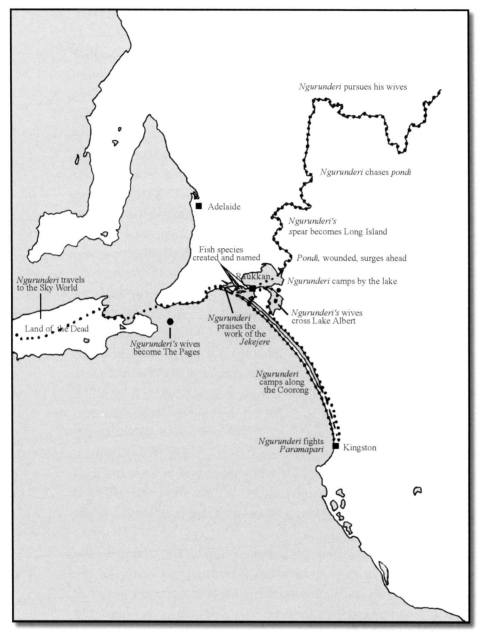

Ngurunderi's Creation Journey Map

The story of the Seven Sisters[14]

At Easter 1998, Aunty Veronica Brodie (1941–2007), respected Ngarrindjeri
Elder, granddaughter of Old Dan Wilson on her father's side, a granddaughter
of George Spender of the Coorong on her mother's side, chose to tell this
segment of the Seven Sisters' story to a select group of female kin (see Bell
1998:578). The story had come to her from her older sister, Aunty Leila
Rankine. When Aunty Leila was dying in 1993, she chose to invest her sacred
women's knowledge in her younger sister (Brodie 2007:145-6). The time was
right. Aunty Veronica had proved she would be a worthy recipient. Then, in
1998, Aunty Veronica deemed it time to pass on some of what she knew. She
chose appropriately related women who had joined her in the struggle to
protect *Kumarangk* and they agreed this text could be made public.

It begins with *Ngurunderi*'s cave that is situated under Signal Point [at Goolwa].
From the cave he looked across to the island. *Ngurunderi* felt it was his responsibility
to look after the sky, the bird life, the waters, because he made the environment
and the island. He was god of the Ngarrindjeri.

His connection with the Seven Sisters was that he sent a young man, Orion,
after the Seven Sisters to chase them and bring them back. They didn't want to
be caught so they headed up to the sky, up and up and over the Milky Way and
hid there and became the Seven Sisters.

When they want to come back to see their Mum, who is still in the waters
– near where the ferry crosses, just a little over towards the mouth, to the south
– there has to be a clear way, so they can return and they'll be returning shortly,
when it gets cold, that's when they disappear from the sky. Then they come back
down and go under the water to be with their mother. Their mother belonged to
the Warrior Women of the Island.

The activities of the Seven Sisters in Ngarrindjeri *ruwi* was contested in 1995
during the Royal Commission into women's religious beliefs and practices.
Where were the sources regarding this story? Where was the evidence that
women had gender-restricted knowledge? The finding of Commissioner Iris
Stevens that a group of Ngarrindjeri women had deliberately fabricated beliefs
to thwart development rested in part on her assertion that the Seven Sisters
story was "never part of the Dreaming of the Ngarrindjeri people" (Stevens
1995:278) and that there was "no tradition or shared belief of Ngarrindjeri
women relating to arcane female practice" (*ibid.*:280) associated with
Kumarangk. But can absence of a written account be evidence of fabrication?

One of the problems with the written historical record is that, for the most part, it was generated by male researchers talking to Ngarrindjeri men and, where they talked to women, they were not able to ask about women's restricted knowledge. Indeed, some were convinced there was no such thing as women's knowledge so there was no need to make any inquiries. Under these conditions, the range of women's stories in the written record is likely to be limited. However, if we read the sources carefully, there are clues. There are references that support and add to the account of Aunty Veronica Brodie's telling of the Seven Sisters story. There are references that attest to the existence of women's ceremonies, albeit from a range of perspectives. There are also multiple versions of some stories and challenges to the written record. Here we focus on sources in which we hear Ngarrindjeri speak, albeit through various filters.

In 1969, Mrs Annie Rankine (1917–1972), known as Aunty Fofon, daughter of Milerum (Clarence Long 1876–1941), a knowledgeable man of the Coorong and Polly Beck (1883–1928) from up River, explained: My father used to tell us children of a special group of stars which is called the Seven Sisters, and before they were moving we weren't allowed to swim because the dandelions were in bloom then, and it was said that when the dandelions are out, the water is still chill, and this is why our people are very strict and don't allow us to swim.

When the flowers all died off and the stars moved over a bit further, this is when we were allowed to swim because in that time the dandelion flowers which cause a fever to anyone would not be out to make us sick. So this is how we were taught the old people's way of living.

Many a time I tried to sneak past, go down to the lake and get away from my dad, but he would be waiting right on the dot for me, and then one whistle from him; we'd know straightaway we had to run, we knew we were wrong. All this will be in my memories and I'll never forget, because it remains so dear to me; taking notice of my father, being brought up that way; this will ever be in my memories.

And that's all I have got to say on the stars.

Over the years a number of other Ngarrindjeri women have commented on the importance of the Seven Sisters. Nanna Lola Cameron Bonney told Liz Tongerie and Steve Hemming that in the Coorong there were initiated women. That means they'd gone through rituals and that means they had stories, Liz said. Nanna Lola is most likely the source of the comment recorded by Philip Clarke (1994:123) that all Aboriginal people were believed to have originated from the Seven Sisters.

Aunty Dodo (1935–2007) was told stories of the stars by her mother's sister, Aunty Rosie Kropinyeri (née Rigney) and made connections between seasonality and the stars (Bell 1998:573–5, 587–91). Aunty Rosie was telling me about the stars, not just the Seven Sisters, but everything in the sky. With the stars at certain times of the year, they knew to move. The stars, the moon, and the sun was like a compass, a calendar, and a clock. They never had watches. They'd move and know that the food could be plentiful when they came back next time after circling around.

Aunty Dodo added another detail to Aunty Fofon's story about not swimming until the dandelions had died off. I remember the old ladies called springtime 'Billy Button time', when the lambs and everything was being born, young birds were coming out you know. Today the appearance of the Seven Sisters in the skies is still keenly anticipated. Aunty Dodo was also told of coming-of-age ceremonies for young Ngarrindjeri *miminar* by her Aunty Rosie but she refused to disclose these stories to the Royal Commission in 1995 (Fergie 1994, 1996) and was found to be a fabricator. Following the dictates of her teaching, when she deemed the time to be right, Aunty Dodo began the process of passing on the knowledge she held in trust from her Aunty Rosie.

"Respect It: Protect It." Banner of Grandmother's Law, Adelaide, August 26, 1998

Photograph: Susan Hawthorne

Ngarrindjeri author, *Minyu* [Grandfather/Great-grandfather] David, as Aunty Dodo always called David Unaipon (1872/3–1967), can be heard on a tape recording of Elaine Treagus (1966) saying that the Seven Sisters (Pleiades) are called *Munjinggi*. In 1925, *Minyu* David wrote of the activities of the *yatukar* [young girls] who become the Pleiades which he spells as *Mungingee*. His story connects the threads of knowledge about stars and women's rituals. Unaipon published many 'legends' of his people and his handwritten notes are lodged in the Mitchell Library.[15] His rhetorical flourishes owe more to his calling as a preacher and his study of the classics than everyday Ngarrindjeri speech but his stories are framed by the activities of the major creative heroes such as *Ngurunderi* and *Nepeli* and *Muntjingga* [Seven Sisters] and are rich in details of Ngarrindjeri *ruwi*. When Aunty Dodo read what *Minyu* David had written she was moved and commented that although the words were different, she could hear Aunty Rosie talking.[16]

In the story of the *Mungingee*, Unaipon (1925) writes:

According to legend it was the *Yartooka* [*Yatukar*] who in the early days of my race, perceived the necessity for the submission of the body to the mind – a submission that would mean the restraint of physical appetite and the effects of pain and fear. They saw that without this there could be no racial advance. Accordingly they presented themselves to the Elders of the tribe for trial by ordeal.

The Elders explained to the *Yartooka* that the test was a difficult one, but the girls were firm in their resolve.

Minyu David details each of the trials endured by the young women as they conquer hunger, pain and fear. Then, he tells us, the leader of the girls stepped forward and addressed all young women.

Yartooka, we have passed through the testings our Elders have prescribed and suffered much pain. Now it is the desire of the Great Spirit that you should go through the same testing. You must know that the selfish person is not happy, because he thinks only of himself. Happiness comes through thinking of others and forgetting self. Greed and pain and fear are caused by thinking too much of self, and so it is necessary to vanquish them. Will you not go and do as we have done?

The *Yartooka* of other tribes eagerly assented, so proud were they of the victory of their sisters.

The Great Spirit was so pleased with them that he sent a great Star Spirit, and the *Yartooka* were transferred to the heavens without death and without further suffering, that they might shine as a guide and a symbol for their race.

On clear nights ever since, the aboriginals look into the skies and revere this wonderful constellation, the *Mungingee*, remembering what the *Yartooka* have done, always thinking of the story of how they were given their seats in the heavens.

Here then are the 'Warrior Women' of Aunty Veronica's story. In the George French Angas 1840s drawing of a young girl, a *yatukar*, the cicatrices are clearly visible on her chest. We don't know the specific story of the marks, but we can see she has been through a rite of passage and that it is most probably a design associated with her *ngatji* that has been inscribed on her body. Nineteenth century artist William Blandowski makes the connection explicit: "All Aborigines have tattoos and by looking at the form of it one can determine ancestry and home of the individual." His 1856–7

Girl of the Lower Murray Tribe near Lake Alexandrina

G.F. Angas 1845, South Australian Museum, Anthropology Archives

sketches show extensive cicatrices on an adult Ngarrindjeri woman whom he identifies as being from the Koorong [Coorong].[17] We might surmise that she has been through both the initial rites and passage for *yatukar* and further ceremonies relevant to her status as an adult woman.

Then, in The Reverend George Taplin's (1873:18) sketch of the culture, we read that the *Mantjingga* is one of the deceased warriors who has gone to heaven along with *Wayungari* (Mars) and *Nepeli* (the brother-in-law of *Ngurunderi*). However, it was not until the 1930s, when South Australian Museum-based ethnologist Norman B. Tindale showed his Ngarrindjeri friend and colleague, Milerum (Tindale 1986), the reference that the identity of the third deceased warrior was clarified. Uncle Clarence Long told Tindale (nd.) that *Mantjingga* means Seven Sisters. Until then readers may have assumed that all warriors were men.

Given the nature of the sources, it is not surprising that we know more of men's practice than we do of women's. Taplin's source was probably

James Ngunaitponi, father of David Unaipon. And, as if to complete the story, Uncle Neville Gollan, when looking at a photograph of James Ngunaitponi, pointed to the cicatrices on his body and identified them as Seven Sisters' dreaming (Bell 1998:584). So now we have a lineage, a transmission of knowledge through the Unaipon line. The father bore the initiation marks that linked him to the story. The son told the story in print and on tape. Ronald Berndt had recorded men's stories about the Seven Sisters in the 1940s (Berndt *et al* 1993:164, 367) from the knowledgeable Albert Karloan. In 1996, Ngarrindjeri men spoke to Justice Mathews of hearing songs of the Seven Sisters in their youth (Bell 1998:583). From these sources, albeit fragmentary, it appears there is a tradition of the Seven Sisters in Ngarrindjeri country. Like many creation stories, there are stories that women know, and stories that men know. There will be a core of shared knowledge, but women and men will have their own ways of elaborating that knowledge in ceremonies. Up until the time of the proposal to build a bridge to *Kumarangk*, there is no evidence that the women were ever asked about the Seven Sisters. Nonetheless there is evidence in the sources of women having ceremonies, women having restricted knowledge and women's bodies becoming part of the landscape.

The strength of the Seven Sisters is evoked in contemporary ceremonial practice. At the October 2–4, 2007 Ngarrindjeri *Miminar* gathering, Rita Lindsay Jr opened the first day by calling upon the Ancestral women to be with her, to cleanse and heal. Rita Lindsay Jr (2008) wrote: I performed the Ngarrindjeri *Memeni Ringbalin*, a traditional women's dance, wearing a belt made from fresh water rushes, feather flowers and string. The belt consists of seven woven circles and seven feather flowers, which represent the Seven Sisters. This woven belt honors the Ancestral women and their place within the *Kaldowinyeri* (the time of creation, the beginning). The belt connected past, present and future through the Ancient Ngarrindjeri art of weaving and as I wore it close to my *mewi*, I felt a strong and close connection to the *waiirri* [the spirit world] and the Ancestral women. I was calling on the Seven Sisters and all Ancestral women to be with us during our gathering.

The design for the Seven Sisters woven belt came to me just before the Ngarrindjeri Women's Gathering, and took two weeks to complete. Feathers are and always have been an integral part of ceremonial decoration. The Feather Flowers on the woven belt were attached using a traditional Ngarrindjeri binding method. My Grandmother Rita Lindsay Sr and my Mother Audrey Lindsay assisted greatly with the binding and plaiting of the string and the attachment of the

left to right: Ngarrindjeri *Miminar Ringbalin*, Rita Lindsay Jr, Camp Coorong, October 2, 2007

Rita carrying a traditional coolamon as part of the healing ritual

Photographs: Vesper Tjukonai

below: Rita leads the gathering as she cleanses at the meeting room with smoke from the ti-tree bush

Photograph: Diane Bell

Rita Lindsay, Ellen Trevorrow, Rita Lindsay Jr, Audrey Lindsay

Photograph: Vesper Tjukonai

Rita returns to the original fire at the conclusion of the ritual

Photograph: Diane Bell

35

'The Seven Sisters', Muriel Van Der Byl,
silk painting, 1996

Photograph: Diane Bell

feathers. Three generations offered a particular skill which was instrumental in the creation of the belt. My grandmother arranged the feather flowers, my mother bound, plaited and attached the feathers and I wove the Seven Sisters Belt. Three generations, three women, honouring the Ancestral women.

Rita Lindsay Jr's performance connects the Seven Sisters story with the *Kaldowinyeri*, her female kin, her *miwi*, and the art of weaving.

The Seven Sisters story is a fascinating puzzle of pieces and there may well be more waiting to be found. Here we have focused on Ngarrindjeri sources from archives, published accounts and current story-telling.

If there were to be a museum exhibit for the Seven Sisters, like the one for *Ngurunderi* in 1989, the following panels might be on display.

Panel One: Who are the Seven Sisters?
- *Mantjingga* are deceased warriors (George Taplin 1873:18).
- *Munjinggi* is the Seven Sisters (David Unaipon to Treagus 1966).
- *Mantjingga* is the Pleiades (Milerum in the 1930s to Tindale and Long n.d.:1).
- *Muntjinggi/Munjinggi/Mungingee* singular? *Muntjinggar/Mantjingga* plural?

Panel Two: Connecting the Seven Sisters with the seasons
- Albert Karloan, recorded 1939–1940, tells of the Pleiades rising in summer and disappearing in Autumn (Berndt *et al* 1993:164, 367).
- Mrs Annie Rankine (1969), Aunty Fofon, echoes Albert Karloan's story and adds the caution, still observed today, about not swimming until the Pleiades are rising.
- Dr Doreen Kartinyeri equates introduced dandelions with native 'Billy Buttons' and the fertility of springtime.

Panel Three: Rituals for Young Women
- David Unaipon's (1924–5) handwritten account of the rites of passage of

young girls (*yatukar*) and the story of the *Mungingee* (Unaipon 1925).
- George French Angas' drawing from the 1840s showing the body scarring of a puberty rite clearly visible on a young girl.
- William Blandowski's 1856–7 drawings of 'tattooed' women of the Coorong.
- Ngarrindjeri women's testimonies (Bell 1998:500ff).

Panel Four: Rituals for Young Men
- Albert Karloan, recorded in 1939–1940, names the *yatukar* as one of the major initiation cycles concerning six girls and one young man (Berndt *et al* 1993:164, 367).
- Ngarrindjeri men talk of seeing the men's Seven Sisters dance in 1996.
- Neville Gollan identifies the cicatrices on James Ngunaitponi as the Seven Sisters, in 1996.

Panel Five: Honouring the Seven Sisters Today
- The struggle to protect *Kumarangk*.
- Aunty Veronica Brodie's story of the Seven Sisters.
- Aunty Ellen Trevorrow's Sister baskets.
- Aunty Muriel Van Der Byl's art work.
- Rita Lindsay Jr dancing *Ngarrindjeri Miminar Ringbalin*.

Sister basket made by Ellen Trevorrow

Photographs: Vesper Tjukonai, 2008

The story of *Wururi*[18]

Ngurunderi is the great connector but there are creative acts that pre-date his arrival in Ngarrindjeri lands. The story of *Wururi*, the huntsman spider *ngatji*, tells how this bad tempered old woman would roam about at night and scatter fires with her digging stick while people slept. When she died there was much happiness and messengers went forth, here and there, with the news. The people – women, men and children – gathered to feast and celebrate. The Ramindjeri ate from her first and as other groups arrived they too ate, each devouring different parts of the body and then each began to speak a distinct language.

Just as the *Ngurunderi Kaldowinyeri* story explains the separation of Kangaroo Island from the mainland, the *ngatji* story of *Wururi* reflects the behaviour of huntsman spiders as recorded by western science. Aspects of the life cycle of the female huntsman spider recorded by Keith McKeown (1936:93–6) include an account of how the huntsman spins a complex, layered, cushioned egg sac that she protects by wrapping it in her legs. Once out of the sac, the spiderlings crowd around their mother and eat pre-digested food from her mouth. Finally, they scatter far and wide. So, in the *Wururi* story, different languages go to different parts of Ngarrindjeri *ruwi* from the body of a female spider *ngatji*, just as food goes into the mouths of everyday huntsmen spiderlings who then scatter far and wide across Ngarrindjeri *ruwi*.

The *Wururi* story is also about the custom of talking to one's *ngatji*. Ron Berndt recorded Albert Karloan as saying: A long time ago *ngatji* [totem] people, the savage *Wururi* now in spider form, climbed up with their legs until they reached the top of a *ngatji* person's head. There they sat comfortably while he spoke to it as it was sitting there (Berndt *et al* 1993:237–8, 454).

Weaving the past and the present

In their everyday activities, art work, and weaving, Ngarrindjeri continue to honour their *ngatji* and their creation stories. Ngarrindjeri who have huntsman spider as their *ngatji* are taught to respect and not to hurt their *ngatji*. Aunty Eileen McHughes (née Kropinyeri) has spider as her *ngatji* on her mother's side and remembers well that her Aunty Pud would never let them harm the huntsman. Aunty Eileen with the bringer of languages as her *ngatji* has become a keen student of her language. In 1987, she obtained her Certificate of Literacy Attainment from the Darwin Institute of Technology and in 2007 completed a module in the Ngarrindjeri language at Technical and Further Education (TAFE) in Murray Bridge as part of her Certificate I in Introducing Vocational Education. Aunty Eileen plans to continue her studies of the Ngarrindjeri language.

Visit the Museum at Camp Coorong and see Audrey Lindsay's painting. Here is the story of her painting as she explained it to Diane in 2007.

I knew basically nothing about the island and I hadn't done any painting for five years before, so it was very significant for me to draw this. I'd been away from the island, up in the Riverland. I had little ones to look after and I was trying to finish my studies, so I hadn't been involved in any of the struggles for *Kumarangk*. Then, it was 2000, we had just moved back and we were camping on the island. The connection was so strong. I just felt it, the connection to the place. The children felt it too. It was the best time of my life, that real feeling. I got the sketch when I was there, on the island, but then we had to move off the island when the bridge was being built. We moved into Meningie and that was where I painted it.

I had it in my head where things were supposed to be placed, like a feeling of how it should be, of how it was. There were huntsman spiders all around at that time and I felt it had to be there, on the island. I spoke to Aunty Sarah Milera and she said it was OK to put the spider there, in the painting, because it was a *ngatji*. "It's OK," she said when I took her the sketch.

On the island, you can see the white lines for the spirit and the red for the blood. The weaving (the wavy lines) are for weaving, not just women's weaving, but they show that everything is connected: land, water, *ngatji*, spirit world, everything. The winding trails that lead towards the island represent where paths cross into other people's territory. They are like guidelines for people and stories. Mundoo Island, next to *Kumarangk*, I had been told was a man's island, so the boomerang is there to symbolise

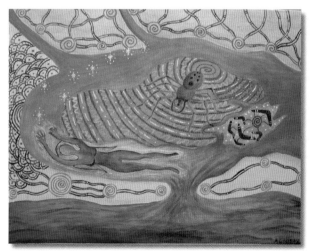

Kumarangk, Audrey Lindsay, Camp Coorong Museum, 2000

Photograph: Diane Bell

man and the spirals are linking and gathering people and their stories together.

The woman in the water is showing the link of the spirit world to our world. There is no break. It's all connected. The mother is in the water waiting for the sisters, the Pleiades. There are eight stars because I just felt there had to be an extra one. Uncle Tom asked me, "Why eight? What was the understanding for that? Was the other one *Ngurunderi*?" I just thought there had to be an extra one. So I painted eight sisters.

At the Murray Mouth the waters mix and change colour. I used a green colour for the water coming through the Mouth and a deep blue for the ocean. You can see where the green and blue mix.

At Goolwa, I tried to get in that area of Signal Point and all that, where the caves were. From there, along the peninsulas, either side of the Murray Mouth, the lines are travelling, getting along on the Hummocks, and showing special places, even all along those sand dunes, special places happen all along there.

Audrey Lindsay paints the connections. They are ones she feels. She confers with Aunty Sarah Milera (née Day, 1947–2006) who was living in Goolwa before proceeding from sketch to painting. Her daughter Rita Jr cleanses the meeting area with smoke from the ritual fire and dances the connections in her Ngarrindjeri *Miminar Ringbalin*. She feels it in her *miwi*. Aunty Eileen McHughes studies the Ngarrindjeri language created by her *ngatji*. Aunty Veronica Brodie passes the story she learned from her sister to the next generation. Aunty Dodo's research connects the generations. Stitch by stitch, circle by circle, says Aunty Ellen Trevorrow. Weaving is like the creation of life, all things are connected.

Caring for Family

Aunty Rosie said: "*Nukan* [look], the way we still do everything in a circle" and I thought, even though she is a long way from home, she still has thoughts about being there, in a circle that's tying us all together... The tightness of the stitches is like the closeness of the family... When you keep adding the fillers, you're adding another member of your family and you don't put them all in together, they're at different stages, just like with family. The family is all different ages, from the tall one down. And when you finish and you're on the last strand of the rush, that is the filling, and when we do it that way, you can't even see where it ends. And that is like the *miwi*, because there is no end to the *miwi*. It's joined on at either end to the placenta and the baby. It's the lifeline.

Aunty Doreen Kartinyeri (Bell 1998:544)

Be a mentor, guide them down the path, but also let them act on what they want to do. Know your children. Know your grannies. Know how they feel about situations.

Kaysha Taylor (2007)

Us women are on the warpath

On June 21, 2007, a day before the first of our workshops at Camp Coorong, the Federal Government announced that it would intervene in the lives of Northern Territory communities because the abuse of children constituted a national emergency (Anderson and Wild 2007). The wide ranging reforms that were proposed included alcohol restrictions; medical examinations of all Indigenous children under the age of sixteen; quarantining 50 per cent of welfare payments to ensure money was spent on food and other essentials; enforcement of school attendance by linking income support and family assistance payments to school attendance; control of townships through five year leases to ensure that property and public housing be improved; on-ground clean-up of communities to make them safer and healthier by marshalling local workforces through Work for the Dole arrangement; scrapping the permit system for common areas and road corridors on Aboriginal lands; banning the possession of X-rated pornography; increasing policing levels; and setting up an Australian Government sexual abuse reporting desk.[19]

The general response from the Ngarrindjeri women was one of outrage and anger. It was not that they disagreed that there were serious problems with policing, employment and housing or that alcohol abuse, pornography, and violence against women and children had to be addressed, but rather that they rejected the notion that the Federal Government could intervene in family life and exclude Aboriginal people from decisions being made about their well-being. It was reminiscent of the 'for their own good' justification of the Stolen Generations and their experience of police and welfare agents who rode into their camps and houses and declared them to be unfit parents. It failed to take account of the initiatives that local communities were proposing, the successful programs that were underway, or the numerous reports and recommendations penned over the past decade.

Here is what the Ngarrindjeri *miminar* had to say: Australia is going backwards. Historically this is what the Europeans did to our ancestors. This government is putting out mixed messages. They say we have the human right to say 'No'. But then they turn around and agree it's OK to traumatise our children and families through health checks. Howard and his Government are traumatising our children. If we were not a violent race before! Don't touch our children's private parts. We've seen the results of interfering with families and our rights as parents before. We want to look after our children. And we want to do it free from government control. Don't tell us this is for our own good. You can look but don't touch if you value yourself because us women are on the warpath. How Dare You?

The women agreed there should be no cover up for child abusers. Expose them for what they are. We want police to catch them and punish them. The perpetrator should be removed from the house, not the victim and children. Give us safe places for victims, resources, compassionate workers. Fix the problem in a humane way. Don't treat Aboriginals as fauna.

Their questions were insistent.

    Who introduced alcohol, drugs and pornography?

    Who tried to take away our culture, lifestyle?

    Why aren't non-Aboriginal children examined as well?

    We don't class all non-Aboriginal people all the same. So why is the
        Australian Government doing it to us?

In the workshops the women said: We need safe places for our children, assistance with relocation to safe places, follow up on abused families, more education of our rights, more education on stranger danger and the confidence to say 'No'. Welfare agencies should be more aware of what is happening to the kids. Families should be educated on what forms they are signing. We need Aboriginal workers to help explain documents and policies. The Government should have more meetings with the Elders on what's happening to the families in their areas, in their communities.

Ngarrindjeri *miminar* identified their safety and well-being, repatriation of the Old People, the Stolen Generations, and substance abuse as central problems and looked to improved housing, education and training, policing, health services and rehabilitation as ways forward. They recognised that their distinctive cultural modes of caring for country and family structured their priorities. They talked about the positive and negative faces of 'feeling shame' and 'being shamed'. They required service providers to be cognisant of Ngarrindjeri culture and to understand their respect for *ngatji*, stories, Elders and the Old People. There was much discussion about how to balance the anger, hurt and need to find ways forward. The general consensus was: It is sad and hurtful to see these issues arising in our communities: drugs, pornography, abuse. But we need to be careful about naming the causes. These things are not part of our culture but the troubles are growing within our communities and we need to take a stand on who is responsible. It's not just us Indigenous people that are having these problems. But we need to acknowledge what is happening, come to terms with the situation and deal with it.

Shame and respect

One evening after a full day of workshops, Aunty Rita Lindsay, Aunty Alice Abdulla, Uncle Tom Trevorrow and Aunty Ellen Trevorrow were talking with Diane Bell about shame as a barrier to success for young women. Shame, said Uncle Tom, can be a good thing. It acts as a kind of protection. We don't make fools of ourselves. But then there's the white man's doing, an imposed shame. Because we were denied equal rights and education, we were not in a position to compete and we feel shame. When young people move beyond the world of family into the education system and into the work place, new rules apply and they feel shamed. They hold back. The Elders were encouraging of the young women, Don't feel shame. Be proud. Aunty Ellen said: It's really important to keep encouraging them. We're going together with what you've got. Share.

Kaysha Taylor reads aloud to the Women's Workshop, Camp Coorong, July 6, 2007

Photograph: Annie Vanderwyk

Kaysha Taylor said: I remember when I was in primary school and I was there with a couple of my first cousins in the same class. The teacher said, "Can you read out loud now?" I used to love reading out loud you know. I'd tell my cousins, don't be shamed, don't walk out of the class. They're not going to know who you are, what you can do. I'd say, "Get up and read." And now I'm at university with them, in a class of 200. It's important for young people in the Adelaide community too. It's important for young Indigenous people not to be too shame, to get up and speak. You're not going to get anywhere otherwise.

Rita Lindsay Jr (2007) wrote: The issue of shame is a curse for our people. What do we have to be ashamed of? We are a beautiful people that come from an ancient race; we are the traditional owners of this land and have a culture to be proud of. I have been subject to being in the situation of shame and I found it to be a method of control and it can prevent you from being who you are and from achieving your goals. Once I overcame this barrier it was an incredible release and sense of freedom. Instead of covering and hiding who we are in mainstream society, I decided to throw light onto the issues that constitute the attitude of being shame and by doing so, I not only helped myself but others also. As a result I set about educating firstly my fellow students, teachers and community about Aboriginal culture and issues affecting Aboriginal people. This was even more meaningful and interesting when I approached Elders within my community because their life experiences, knowledge and wisdom were fundamental to my growth, personal, academically and culturally. What I need to say to other women is that you can have any future you want, it just takes commitment and dedication and it will all be worth it in the end.

Aunty Ellen Trevorrow, who has demonstrated and taught weaving across Australia and in North America recalled a time when she had felt shame: I was in a lecture theatre where the seats went up to the back of the room, in steps. I was weaving, sharing, but it was like they was looking down on me in that lecture theatre. I was shamed. Then I moved to another location and I was on the same level and I felt at ease. It happened in between the two locations. I was shamed and then I was OK.

Aunty Eileen McHughes added: When you use the word 'shame', it's not really shame, it's more ashamed you're Aboriginal and people can look down on you and you'll make mistakes. Very few will praise you. They're more likely to put you down. We were taught to call ourselves 'half-castes', her sister Vicki Hartman adds. Later that evening a number of the Elders began to compile a list. We were called Boongs, Coons, Abos, Niggers, Blackfellas, Half-castes and Breeds. We were told to go back where we came from – Africa – this isn't your country. A common story of families divided by the colour line: My Mum was between my husband and me in terms of colour and she was classed as a 'full-blood' and Dad, who was darker, was classed as a 'half-caste'. So what sense does that make? Well it makes a difference in terms of where you can travel and how your kids identify.

Our children

Being able to care for their children and keep them safe from danger is stressed in Ngarrindjeri traditional story-telling where a number of cautionary tales counsel mothers to watch their children and warn children away from dangerous places. In the story of the *prupi* at McGraths Flat, a bad-tempered old woman steals children (Tindale 1938). Children are warned not to swim in the River until the dandelions have died off in case they get yellow fever (Rankine 1969). They are taught to keep away from deep places in the River Murray for fear the *mulyawongk* will take them and naughty children are told the *mulyawongk* will come and get them (Hemming 1985).

Ngarrindjeri *miminar* have taken an active role in asserting their rights as parents to care for their children. In 1923, three Ngarrindjeri Elders presented the 'Give us our children' petition to the Governor of South Australia. The petition opposed the passage of the *Aborigines (Training of Children) Act 1923* that legalised the removal of children. On behalf of Ngarrindjeri mothers, preacher Grandfather Edward Norman Kropinyeri, husband of Granny Ellen Kropinyeri (née Sumner) wrote:

This Act, like a mysterious creature of ill omen, is casting a gloom over this one little mission home. Yes, this Bill has passed at last, and the passing of it provides food for serious consideration. And the first that presents itself to the mind, is the fact that, an Act, which, hitherto had been illegal and I believe, punished by law, is now legal and supported by law, which produces a reverse effect upon the past legal law, as for instance, in the past any one taking a child away from its parents without their consent, will be liable to punishment by law. But today, any desiring to return and live with their parents, will be dealt with by the laws contained in the Act. Here we have a queer conglomeration of laws, through some unaccountable way, the wild cat of confusion, has effected or gained an entrance into the dovecote of legal harmony, and caused such utter confusion among the inmates, to such an extent, that some, if not all, of them cannot with any degree of accuracy, claim each their respective relationship either to the legal, or illegal origin. However this is not the matter on which I wish to write. It is mother's love, its claims, its rights, its demands. Now it is understood that a refusal to comply with the demands of an ultimatum of one nation to another, is an acceptance of condition of warfare whatever those conditions may lead to, so the passing of that Bill is a declaration of war between right and wrong. And there is only one right, and only one wrong, which of the two contending party [sic] is right. We will see presently. Mark well, the two forces, arrayed against each other. There stands the advocates, and supporters of the Bill that has passed, strongly fortified, their guns of 'intellect' trained and ready for action, they represent 'Right'. There, on the opposite and facing them is the rank of the enemy, strongly opposing the Bill, a very strange army, possessing no weapons of war, no intellectual powers, no Parliamentary eloquence, not a grain of science in the whole body, that makes the army of motherhood. The only piece of artillery which that army possesses is the weapon called love. And thus equipped, the army of motherhood has taken up their position in opposition to the Bill. The invader of those Godgiven and therefore sacred dominions of mother's love is its claims, its rights, its demands, a possessin [sic] voted for them in the parliament of heaven, sealed with the image and superstition of His Majesty, whose name is 'Love'. This army also represents Right.

Thus we see the two contending forces each striving for precedence in their claim of Right, and we ask, who is going to win the day? And the reply comes from the ranks of Intellect, "victory is ours", and relying on their weapon of attack, Intellect, they thunder forth their intellectual arguments again and again, propelled by the full force of scientific facts. Poor motherhood, how are you going to retain the beauties and glorious possession of motherhood, the right, the claims, the demands of love amid such fearful intellectual bombardment as this, and seeing that you are armed with nothing more than the crude and primitive weapon, love, the invention of which dates back in the past eternity. It is true we are indeed poorly equipped, and we know not how we are going to fare in this fearful struggle, but – and just then a thin spurt of smoke is seen issuing from the ranks of motherhood, and we knew that love, motherhood's weapon spoke, and that its claims, its demands, and its rights, in their threefold unity is speeding its unerring way to the ranks of the foe, bearing the seal, the hallmark, and the mandate of the majesty on high (the majesty of love). Hon. members (jurymen). The question is asked, Who wins? The bar of eternal justice, truth and righteousness awaits your verdict! What say you?

Point McLeay. December 16, 1923

Tom Trevorrow takes up the story of the remarkable petition in his introduction to *They took our land and then our children* (Trevorrow *et al* 2007). Questions were raised by the Ngarrindjeri to the Government as to the outcome or whereabouts of the 1923 petition that our Elders delivered to the Government, but sadly the Government could not find the Petition and did not know the outcome or whereabouts of the petition. Its existence was known via a reference in an index to South Australian newspapers but it was the microfiche copy of the document found in 2002 by Flinders University postgraduate researcher Karen Hughes and shown to Aunty Ellen and Uncle Tom Trevorrow at Camp Coorong that revived interest in the petition.

On December 17, 2003, three Ngarrindjeri ambassadors, Uncle Neville Gollan, Uncle Marshall Carter and Daryle Rigney re-presented the petition to Her Excellency, Marjorie Jackson-Nelson, then Governor of South Australia in a re-enactment of the 1923 presentation. With the support of a number of bodies including the Ngarrindjeri Heritage Committee, Steve Hemming of Flinders University, Patrick Byrt of the Roma Mitchell Community Legal Service, the Migration Museum, a division of the History Trust of South Australia, the Department of Aboriginal Affairs and Reconciliation and the Department of Families and Communities, the petition became the centre piece of an exhibit of panels officially launched in Victoria Square, December 10, 2004. The book, *They took our land and then our children*, which includes these panels, was launched by Uncle Tom Trevorrow at the Migration Museum on National Sorry Day, May 26, 2007.

Along with the re-presentation of the petition on December 17, 2003, a further delegation of Uncle Tom and Aunty Ellen Trevorrow, Uncle George Trevorrow and Uncle Matt Rigney presented Her Excellency with the 'Proclamation of Ngarrindjeri Dominium' (see Chapter Four and Appendix Two).

The Ngarrindjeri continue their struggle for justice. On August 1, 2007, they made legal history when Bruce Trevorrow, brother of Aunty Hilda, Uncle George, Uncle Tom, Aunty Rita, Aunty Alice, Uncle Cyril, Uncle Victor, Aunty Karen, Uncle Devon, Uncle James, and Uncle Joseph became the first member of the Stolen Generations to receive compensation. In explaining his reasons for the decision, The Honourable Justice Thomas Gray of the Supreme Court of South Australia (Gray 2007) spoke of the strength of the Trevorrow family and in giving evidence Aunty Alice and Aunty Rita had recounted the commitment of their mother, Thora Lampard, to finding her baby and having him returned to her care.

Aunty Thora's story

Aunty Thora Lampard sought the return of her son, Bruce Trevorrow. On 25 July 1958, she wrote to Mrs Angas, a welfare officer in the Aborigines Department (Gray 2007:para 125).

> I am writing to ask if you will let me know how baby Bruce is and how long before I can have him home as I have not forgot I got a baby in there and I would like something defenat [sic] about him this time trust you will let me know as soon as possible.
>
> Yours faithfully [Thora]
> Meningie.

The response from the secretary of the Aborigines Protection Board (APB) on August 19, 1958, advised that baby Bruce was making good progress but that the doctor did not yet consider him fit to go home.

The facts, Justice Gray found in his August 1, 2007 judgment, were at odds with this account from the APB. He wrote: "The reference to the suggested views of 'the doctor' finds no direct or indirect support from any evidence led at trial. Having reviewed the evidence, I am satisfied that there was no medical advice as suggested" (Gray 2007:para 127). Having heard from many Ngarrindjeri witnesses and having had access to a range of archival material, Justice Gray (paras 1–2) found that on Christmas Day 1957, 13-month-old baby Bruce was driven by neighbours from Meningie to the Adelaide Children's Hospital where he was admitted. The hospital notes recorded that he had no parents and that he was neglected and malnourished. According to the hospital records, baby Bruce responded to treatment and by New Year's Eve it was noted that he was "going well". On January 6, 1958, Martha Davies, having responded to a newspaper advertisement seeking foster care for Aboriginal babies, saw baby Bruce and decided to take him home. This process was authorised and arranged by an officer of the Aborigines Department on behalf of the APB. Thora Lampard did not see her son again until almost a decade later. His father, Joseph Trevorrow never saw his son again. He died some eight years after his son was stolen.

Justice Gray (2007:para 299) wrote: "Thora was a loving mother. She loved and cared for her children and step-children. She did her best to provide for the children. This included their emotional, material and educational needs. A number of witnesses spoke about Thora, in particular, her children and step-children". Aunty Rita Lindsay was about seventeen and no longer living at home when her brother Bruce was stolen. She spoke of her step-mother Thora in the following terms (*ibid.*:para 304).

A. Well, she was very good to us. She made sure that we got a little bit more education, to finish school off, as much as we can and she'd help us and she was pretty good to us. No complaints.

Q. Did she teach you things.

A. Yes, how to cook and you know and sew clothes.

Q. How did she sew clothes.

A. Needle and cotton.

Q. There wasn't any power at One Mile.

A. No.

Q. What else did she teach you.

A. Just basic things, you know; when us girls were getting older.

Q. Women's sorts of things.

A. Yes, women's.

Q. You saw her around her children, around Hilda, then George, then Tom. You saw her look after them.

A. Yes, yes.

Q. Can you tell us about how she was around the babies.

A. She was a sort of a loving mother. She took pretty good care of them while I was, you know, around.

Aunty Alice Abdulla was aged about fifteen years old at the time of her brother's removal. She described living with Joseph and Thora from about 1954 (Gray 2007:para 307).

Q. Can you tell his Honour about what kind of mother she was with young children.

A. She was caring and loving with the children, the same as she was with us when I was living there and going to school.

Q. What things would she do with the children. What special things would she do for you and your sisters and brothers.

A. As I said, besides teaching us how to cook and sew and everything, she would check our books, what we had for school, make sure we kept up-to-date with everything and just the normal, you know, caring mother.

Q. Would she do anything special on birthdays.

A. Yes, birthdays were very special, a special treat for all of us. I mean, living in the camps we didn't have much treats, it was very hard for all of us kids, but what we had we valued, you know, treats like that.

In his Conclusion, Justice Gray (paras 1228–1230) wrote:

> The plaintiff, as an infant and as a child, was dealt with by the State without lawful authority in a manner that affected his personal well being and freedom. He was the subject of misfeasance in public office. He was falsely imprisoned. He was the subject of breaches of the common law duty of care owed by the State…

> The parents of the plaintiff were unaware of what was occurring. They did not consent. The plaintiff's mother was provided misinformation about her son. It was a serious matter that contact between the natural family and the plaintiff, and in particular, between the plaintiff and his mother, was obstructed and did not occur for almost a decade. These circumstances left the plaintiff, as a child, suffering from an anxiety state, depression and illnesses associated with depression.

It was not only Bruce whose life was shattered. As his older sister Aunty Rita Lindsay commented: I remember Dad brought Bruce to his neighbour's house to ask for a lift, he didn't have a car, and he had Bruce wrapped up in a government blanket, all warm. I can see his little face and curly hair. "He's got a bit of a stomach ache," Dad said. "We'll take him," they said. I was working and had to go back at 2.30pm. Thora was away and when she came back a couple of days later – she'd heard Bruce had been taken to hospital – I could see the look in her face, "What's happened to my son?" We couldn't get any information out of the department. It was starting to rock us all. I could see the anguish in Thora's face, "I've really lost him." She said, "It's never happened before." And why should it? The next time we saw him was in Kintore St at Aboriginal Affairs. I was so happy but he was shy. He didn't know anything about me. I can still see that little face and curly hair.

What happened to Bruce sort of put me off life a bit. I went a bit off track. When I found out what Aboriginal Affairs was doing, I realised they could have done that to anyone. Stealing children is like grave robbing. I class them as thieves. We wanted the message from the hospital to pick him up, but no message came. We were sitting up all night, worrying how is he going? It had a big impact on our family. And on me. To think as a mother, if I was away and my child was sick, the child could be taken. It made me more protective of my own children. One lesson was you just can't trust a white person in a high position. Bruce missed out on learning respect for Elders. Dad missed out on seeing Bruce by several years. It would have been different if only he had seen his father.

On June 23, 2007, Will Trevorrow, the great-nephew of Bruce Trevorrow, turned one. At Camp Coorong, families visit, camp, attend meetings and workshops, tell stories, organise trips. Children, grannies [grandchildren], cousins, nieces and nephews play under the watchful eyes of their Elders. The family was there to help Will celebrate.

Will Turns One, Camp Coorong, June 23, 2007

Grandparents: Pop Tom and Nanna Ellen Trevorrow; Will Trevorrow; Great Aunt: Noreen Kartinyeri; Great Aunt: Glenda Rigney (holding Will); Cousin: Dylan Gibbs Trevorrow (in front), and Parents: Tamara Biddle and Luke Trevorrow.

Photograph: Diane Bell

Aunty Veronica's story

The tragedy of children denied the love of the "army of motherhood" cited in the 1923 petition has left deep scars on Ngarrindjeri families. In *My Side of the Bridge*, Aunty Veronica Brodie takes up the issue of the Stolen Generations as she tells the story of two of her nephews who were taken from their mother at Raukkan, of how their mother was tricked into signing adoption papers she thought were for temporary fostering, of the name changes of the boys and their struggle in coming to terms with the truth of their removal and adoption (2007:163–175). She writes: English was the only thing they ever learnt in schools, so when they got older they weren't able to relate back to their people and culture… We've got kids who have suicided because they can't cope in a mixed world … They get lost (2007:163).

Telling the stories is no light matter. On November 7, 2004, Veronica Brodie told her story (Trevorrow *et al* 2007).

It was back in the early 1950s. I was about 13 years old, living at Raukkan.

The big black car pulled up outside a house, a welfare officer entered the house. About 10 minutes later the officer came out with four children and shoved them into the car.

The mother came out screaming, crying, pulling at her hair. Falling down on her knees in the dust and dirt screaming and crying. Her children were on the back seat screaming and crying, looking at their mother as they drove off.

I recall standing there in fear with tears running down my cheeks and saying, "My God! What did that woman just do."

The eldest son of that family is still alive today. He says not a day goes by when he doesn't recall that time in his life and his emotions turn to sadness and hatred.

He never saw his mother alive again.

Aunty Veronica's older sister, Aunty Leila Rankine, writing in 1974 of life on Raukkan in the 1960s and of the restrictions placed on families, explains how difficult it was for families to be together: Every Aboriginal man, woman and child had to have a permit stating that he was allowed to reside on the Reserve. It was also necessary to get permission from the Superintendent, or duty officer, if former residents wished to have their deceased relatives buried on the Reserve, or to attend a funeral. Visitors and children of residents, visiting on weekends, had to report to a duty officer on arrival. When my fourth child, now ten years of age, was two weeks old, two members of the Government Department approached me as to whether or not I had a permit for her to live with me. When I told them I didn't have one, they then informed me that my child could be removed from my care. I told them they could do their hardest and the only way they would get my child would be over my dead body. To date I haven't heard any more of this.

At the August 2007 workshop, having talked at length about the Bruce Trevorrow case and the experience of the Stolen Generations, the women declared: As Ngarrindjeri women we urge the SA Government to move forward and to find a way to put a package in place to address issues for other stolen children. The stories are being told and, as Doris Kartinyeri explains in *Kick the Tin* (2000), they are part of a journey of healing. One critical step in this journey was for the Australian Government to say sorry.

On February 13, 2008, the Prime Minister, Kevin Rudd, took this step when he apologised to the Stolen Generation and their families. He apologised for the laws that had caused the pain and suffering and he apologised for the indignity and degradation inflicted on a proud people and culture (see Apology, inside back cover). Ngarrindjeri were present in the Gallery of Parliament House and on the lawns outside. They watched in their communities, at home, at work and in Elder Park in Adelaide. The mood was positive and forward-looking.

> It was a long time coming but this is a first step to healing.
>
> It took a really great man to take on the burden of saying sorry for all past injustices.
>
> Remember we have problems in the urban areas too. It's not just remote communities.
>
> We've been waiting for this moment. My first reaction was tears, then celebration.
>
> It's a way of moving us forward with Reconciliation, especially for our young ones.

What to do now? Australia needs to sign the Universal Declaration of the Rights of Indigenous Peoples. We need a Bill of Rights to protect all people.

Then on February 28, 2008, the State of South Australia appealed the judgment of Justice Gray to the Full Court of the Supreme Court of South Australia. The appeal was against the whole of the judgment that included damages in the sum of $525,000 and the sum of $250,000 in interest.[20] The Premier, Mike Rann (2007) had said at the time of the August 1, 2007, judgment that the compensation would not be appealed but left room for an appeal against precedent-setting aspects of the decision. In commenting on the February 28, 2008 appeal, the South Australian Attorney-General Michael Atkinson (2008a, b) stressed the need to clarify the law with respect to the Stolen Generations and reiterated that the state would not seek to challenge the compensation awarded by Justice Gray. An appeal puts other claims for compensation on hold and significantly undermines the Federal Apology to the Stolen Generations.

Our Old People

> Let them rest, that is our plea.

On Saturday September 23, 2006, twenty-four Old People who, in the name of science, had been taken from their burial grounds by South Australian Coroner William Ramsay Smith in the decade 1898–1908 and held for nearly a century in the Museum at Edinburgh University, Scotland, were returned to their *ruwi* at *Warnung* [Hack's Point] and Parnka Point on the Coorong (Hemming 2006; Hemming and Wilson in press; Wallis *et al* 2006; Wilson 2005). There are some 400 more Old People awaiting proper burial at Camp Coorong and thousands more yet to be repatriated to Ngarrindjeri country.

We want them home, where they can rest.

We need support for the families, compensation, assistance with the costs.

There are a number of references about the importance of being able to do proper ceremonies for those who have passed away. In the 1940s, Albert Karloan explained to the Berndts that the spirit would come back "tormented" looking for the dead unless the belongings are located and buried (Berndt *et al* 1993:16, 510). The grannies are taught this today. In Aunty Maggie's story it is emphasised that Aunty Leila always said she wanted to go back to the Coorong to die. That was where she felt at home.

The Old People must be retuned to their appropriate area. They deserve the same respect as non-Indigenous persons, said Aunty Eileen McHughes. Burial sites are of very spiritual importance to Ngarrindjeri people. Our belief is that their spirits won't rest if buried in the wrong area. We don't just respect the living, we also respect those who have passed away.

There are ceremonies which must be conducted before the Old People can be moved from the vaults and boxes and bags in which they are currently stored in various museums in Australia and overseas and transported back to Ngarrindjeri *ruwi*. There are ceremonies to be conducted once they are home. These ceremonies require planning and resources. The preparations for the September 2006 reburials took months and involved many.

At the workshops, the women enumerated their requirements:

- Time for organising and preparation
- Assistance in locating the appropriate official channels to release the 'remains'
- Access to information and the right documentation
- Being able to do the appropriate ceremonies
- Elders to go overseas, with traditional family escorts, travel first class, do the smoking ceremony over there and do a cleansing ceremony when they arrive home
- Access to appropriate areas, sacred grounds for reburials
- Informing the family and communications
- Making sure proper postage and handling is done correctly.

We urgently need resources so that correct, proper, right ceremonies at the right places can be done and the Old People can be where they belong, said Aunty Rita Lindsay and Aunty Alice Abdulla who had done much of the women's work required before the reburial. Diane: "I worked with Aunty Rita making the coffins. Using the tools and skills used in the manufacture of feather flowers, we wired wattle and ti-tree to the outside of the coffins. When the little coffins were complete, along with all the women who had helped, we walked single file through the smoke from the burial platform built outside the repatriation room and placed the coffins on the long tables that were covered with black cloth. It was a solemn moment."

Across the generations

The generation who grew up in the fringe camps emphasise the sharing and making do: aunts, uncles, and grandparents were part of their daily routines. They had mothers, sisters, aunts and cousins close by to help with child-rearing, food gathering, and dispute resolution, and to keep them safe. In her story, Aunty Eileen McHughes talked about being surrounded by family at the Three Mile Camp at Tailem Bend. In this way she was surrounded by stories of the past and mentored as a young woman by her female kin. Her mother died when the youngest of her family was only five but Eileen was not alone. There were others to share the load. The discipline was strict but it was in the open. These days, the privatisation of the family as a two generational unit living in a space hidden from other family members, places enormous strain on young couples. We don't know what happens behind closed doors, one young woman complained. We want to know what you think. What do you feel? We only see you crying at funerals. But what do you feel about what is happening now? If we knew we were upsetting you, we'd be shamed.

What was it like for you Mum? younger women asked. The older women talked about life in the fringe camps of Meningie and Tailem Bend. When we lived in the fringe camps, we were all together, all sharing. No fences, no closed doors, Aunty Rita Lindsay recalled. At sundown, we'd see the smoke from everyone's camp. It was very comforting. We looked out for each other but the Council wanted to start moving us. We had to be more than a mile out of town. That's when we moved to the Three Mile Camp.

While these caring mothers do help to care for their grannies, there were complaints that the line between being a mother and a grandmother was

Pelicans led the way, *Warnung*, September 23, 2006

Photograph: Diane Bell

Inside the repatriation room, Camp Coorong, September 20, 2006

Photograph: Diane Bell

Major Sumner and Doug Nicholls Jr at the reburial site for the Old People, *Warnung*, September 23, 2006

Photograph: Diane Bell

Cleansing fire, Coorong, September 23, 2006

Photograph: Diane Bell

The Old People being carried by their kin to their resting place on their *ruwi*, September 23, 2006

Steven Roberts, Christopher Roberts, Bill Karpany Sr, Laurie Rankine Sr, Christian Aspel, Joe Trevorrow.

Photograph: Diane Bell

blurred. Edie Carter said: They're around 24/7 but I don't get time to hear from Mum, we don't get time to yarn. We've been too busy with study and relationships and now we have kids. My Mum says, "I'm a mum and a grandmother trying to play a grandmother role." Her mother, Millie Rigney, interjected, But grandmothers are supposed to love the grannies and hand them back. I tell my grannies, "I'm not your mother. I'm your Nanna." That's what I tell the grannies. Edie: If you're working, like I am, Mum is trying to be that mother role. But Mum, you're a single grandmother and an aunty out to the community as well. Millie: There are lots of things inside our hearts, things that we have not yet spoken to our kids, to our nieces and nephews. That's the really painful part.

Edie Carter, Kaysha Taylor, Donna Kartinyeri, Dorothy Kartinyeri, Georgina Trevorrow and Rita Lindsay Jr expressed their dismay as young women at the level of violence within their communities. They identified drugs, racism, families broken by Stolen Generation practices and lack of education as key factors. This generation is well educated, well travelled and technologically adept. They have enormous respect for their Elders, cherish their Ngarrindjeri networks and want to be part of building a strong nation.

Edie Carter talked at length about a DVD made by the Grannies Group in Adelaide that featured Ngarrindjeri Elders. It really impacted on me when I saw the aunties from our community talking about how they felt about the drugs. What we put our mothers and grandmothers through! That really impacted on me. This was the first time I'd seen my aunties telling their stories, talking about personal issues. Aunty Veronica was there, crying, talking about her life. On the DVD you hear them say, "I've told my kids not to come back here anymore if they're using." And I'm imagining what they're feeling and what the Elders are thinking and how others in the community are feeling. That's a lot of shame. I know it took them ten years to make that DVD, but I'll put my hand up to work on one here. I want the stories to be told.

Edie's words hit the spot. The younger women talked about all the things they wanted to know, all the things they wanted to ask their Elders. Individual women cried as they pleaded, Tell us about how the families are related. We want to know who we can go with and who we can't. The Elders pieced together knowledge of various lineages and talked with each other during the morning tea-break about who had lived with whom, where and when. These conversations continued throughout that day and well into the night.

In the workshop, the young women's questions kept coming as they began to talk about the ways in which the issue of drugs was dealt with in their families. Here are some of their comments.

When I saw my aunties and Nanna crying, I thought, if that is how my Nanna is going to think about me, and I've got all the respect in the world for my Nanna, I'm going to back away from drugs.

Tell us how you feel? About drugs, about relationships, about us?

Mum tells me how she feels about alcohol and kids coming to the house. But do all kids have that relationship with their parents? We've had our arguments. But we love each other. We never part in anger, well not for long. I walked out of an argument once and five minutes later I phoned to say sorry and I love ya.

My Mum is a real role model for me.

Tell us what it was like when you were growing up?

The Elders spoke of their days growing up in the fringe camps.

The only thing I used to do was drink, no drugs, they weren't available then. Now the pushers give them away, free drugs, get the kids hooked, and then it's too late. They come looking for money.

I've lost one daughter to drugs. I hold it inside. It hurts. I want to put the dealers inside.

My son was using and I offered to drive him around one day when he was after drugs. I wrote down the addresses and registration numbers of the dealers and took them to the police, but nothing happened. That policeman left town and didn't come back.

A lot of time you feel shame. You think you've been a good parent and then you see the kids on drugs and I don't like it.

Aunty Eileen McHughes had the final word, Look, there was genocide before and now, you fellars, it's happening again. You're making white fellars rich.

The Grannies Group DVD was shown at the Ngarrindjeri *Miminar* Gathering at Camp Coorong. The six featured story-tellers – Gloria, Veronica, Diana, Heather, Coral and Isabelle – endorse the group's goal: We want grandmothers to be able to be grandmothers. They speak of their first hand knowledge of the devastation of drug use in their families and communities, of children lost to drugs and children pulled back from the brink of self-destruction. They speak of their work in various community-based organisations and most particularly of their children and grandchildren.

As their website[21] explains: The Grannies Group was established in 1999 as a support group of Aboriginal grandparents who advocate on behalf of the children, grandchildren and community. Aunty Gloria, born at Raukkan in

Mother and daughter: Audrey Lindsay and Rita
Lindsay Jr, Camp Coorong, August 19, 2007

Photograph: Diane Bell

Grandmother, daughter and grannies: Innes Jackson
holding Peter Jackson, Brendon Jackson (sitting),
Phoebe Kartinyeri (standing), Helen Jackson (sitting),
Camp Coorong, August 19, 2007

Photograph: Diane Bell

Mother and
daughters: Edie
Carter, Lotoya and
Harmony Love,
Camp Coorong,
August 19, 2007

Photograph:
Diane Bell

1940 has eleven grandchildren and three great grandchildren. She says, I love every one of them so much, I live for them all. Aunty Coral, born Point Pearce in 1937, has worked in Correctional Services and for the Port Adelaide Council. She has 40 grandchildren and 45 great grandchildren. I like working with people, she says. The women spoke of the strengths and distinctively Ngarrindjeri ways of caring for families. It's the multi-generational families and the web of kin who care for children that is not easily understood by child care agencies.

The young women were forthright and articulate. Edie Carter: I want others to see this DVD. I want something to be done. We can talk about a rehabilitation centre here but if we don't push it, it won't happen. I'll put my hand up to do something. Kaysha Taylor prepared a list: On my list, I have requests for what I'd like my grandchildren to do in the future. My request would be, take control and responsibility, be in their lives as they are in yours. Be a mentor, guide them down the path, but also let them act on what they want to do. Know your children. Know your grannies. Know how they feel about situations. How would you like them to act? And from my perspective, I'd like to sit down with my grandmother and hear old stories of her growing up on the mission and her family and what she did all the time and how different that is from my generation: no driving around in cars, no going shopping on the mission. Her fun thing was swimming in the creek. I find these personal stories really interesting. Children of my age try their best. I think they would enjoy hearing those stories as much as the grandparents might enjoy stories coming from the grannies.

When Audrey Lindsay rose to speak she was holding back the tears. I missed the opportunity to talk to my grandma. You don't know what you've lost til they're gone, how important it really is to record it, make a video. Later, when she had read this section, she told Diane, I was all right until I thought about my grandma and then I could see her face, I lost it. Audrey's plea did not go unanswered. Her Aunty Alice responded. This is what I'd tell you young ones about the camps, the One Mile Camp and the Three Mile Camp. I'd talk about relationships in the camps, communicating with the Elders and the aunties. That's where the discipline came in. I'd talk about how my parents separated and how I coped in later years and about finding out about who my parents really were and being really happy because there was love on both sides. I'd tell about how we spent our youth and compare it to now. There's a big difference. We need to communicate more with our youth, in groups, or one on one if they wanted it.

There needs to be respect. It works both ways. I can honestly say I get a great

Grandmother, daughter and grannies: Eileen McHughes (grandmother) Georgia (granddaughter), Georgie Trevorrow (daughter) and Jacob (grandson), Camp Coorong, August 19, 2007

Photograph: Diane Bell

Sisters, mother and aunt: Donna and Dorothy Kartinyeri, with mother Noreen Kartinyeri and her sister Thelma Smart, Camp Coorong, August 19, 2007

Photograph: Diane Bell

Baby Glen Gayford with Aunt Hilda Day, January 2006

Photograph: Vesper Tjukonai

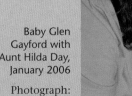

61

deal of respect around here from them all, so I'm lucky. I try to be a role model. Sometimes I let my hair down, like we all do. But I like to try to stay encouraging with them, with their needs, even if it's emotional, or connected to drugs and all that. It doesn't always work, but maybe we've planted a seed there. We know it will spring forth.

I'd be telling stories about the Willy wagtail and the *mingka* bird and what it means to us when we see it, everything going on all around us. In the River and how important it is to us and the animals. We can all get educated together, learn from one another.

As Aunty Alice sat down, there was a round of applause and general agreement that we needed morning tea. The stories kept coming.

Georgie Trevorrow, Aunty Vicki Hartman and Aunty Eileen McHughes said, As women we care what the future holds for our families and children. We need to be serious about caring for our children and grandchildren and so on. We need every family member to put aside their differences and work together as a united group. Of her early life Aunty Eileen said, By 1952, our family had moved from the Three Mile Camp into Tailem Bend where my father got a job on the railways and we moved into a railway house. We were all in school there. When I turned fourteen, I got a job as a domestic, then worked at the Road House and Bakery. I wanted an education. I was strong-minded about things. I got that from my mother. I'd never let anyone put me down.

Email Stories

At the workshops the stories were all oral and while younger women like Edie Carter and Kaysha Taylor spoke at length, several of the other young women were distracted by their child care responsibilities and suggested they write their stories and communicate by email. They wanted time to think about what they would say. They wanted to share what they had already written on a number of the issues in assignments as part of their education, in speeches they had delivered and in reports on programs they had undertaken. So, after four workshops, hours of note taking and tape transcription, the stories emailed to Diane Bell from Dorothy and Donna Kartinyeri (2007), Rita Lindsay Jr (2007), Kaysha Taylor (2007) and Georgie Trevorrow (2007) were added to the Ngarrindjeri *miminar* stories.

On the subject of young women's concerns, sisters Dorothy and Donna Kartinyeri (2007), who work at Meningie in the CDEP (Community

Development Employment Program), doing book-keeping and administration work, wrote of two related issues – the abuse of drugs, and lack of education for young people.

We don't have enough Aboriginal kids staying at school and completing year 12, which is very important indeed.

For us, we would like to see our young talented students completing school, being successful and getting a job, but we feel that there is a need of more positive role models for this to happen.

We need to be more involved with our children's education/learning, supporting and encouraging them every step of the way. We need more Aboriginal workers in child-care, kindys, schools and TAFE [Technical and Further Education] and Uni.

For Georgie Trevorrow, family is at the core of everything she does, at home and at work. At the workshops, she always sat with her mother and mother's sister. Her daughter, Georgia, played under the watchful eyes of her

female kin. Georgie Trevorrow (2007) wrote:

Families are a big part of my life. I love my children, my husband, my parents, in-laws and my relatives and if I don't have them in my life I feel as though I have nothing in this world. I need to be part of this family Nation to keep our culture alive because that is important to me and my family.

I work two days a week for Families SA as a Case Support Worker in the Aboriginal Family Team. And I work three days a week at Murray Mallee Community Health Service as an Aboriginal Children and Families Program Worker.

At Families SA, I case-manage Aboriginal children who are under Guardianship of the Minister.

At Murray Mallee Community Health, I'm linking into current programs that are already running in the Murray Bridge, Meningie and Raukkan area. I will be supporting playgroups in Murray Bridge and Meningie. I will be attending a meeting at the Raukkan school/kindy to see what programs they run or what they would like to have running.

I will also be advocating for Aboriginal families and offering support when needed.

As an Aboriginal worker at Families SA, I would like to do more community work in the prevention area, as it makes me so sad to have our children in the welfare system, sometimes some of them are short term but the majority of them are long term and may even get lost in the system.

My concern as a young Ngarrindjeri woman is that we are going backwards instead of forwards because of the government. I feel as though our Elders have been fighting the government for so long that their health deteriorates and we no longer have them. There is so much illness in the world today that takes the lives of our people, like diabetes, heart disease, mental illness and then the drugs that our people continue to use even with so many deaths.

Rita Lindsay Jr (2007) emailed a number of attachments documenting her activities, travels, inspirational speeches and hopes for the future.

What do I want to do? I aim to educate people through the areas of music, art, and literature, as well as oral teaching, just as the Ancestors did thousands of years ago, which the Elders are teaching in contemporary society. I want to become successful and pursue a career in Athletics, Music and Art, to set an example and to be a role model and leader, so that my people receive recognition also.

As the younger generation, we are obliged to take the initiative and keep the culture alive through traditional dance, traditional arts and crafts and displaying leadership qualities, and so on. We owe it to our Old People, our Ancestors, and our Elders who fought for years for the benefit of our future, til the last breath in their bodies. If we, the younger generation, do not continue what our Elders have fought tirelessly for, then all that they have done would have been in vain. The younger generations are the future and it is our responsibility as Ngarrindjeri people, the custodians of our land and the descendants of our Old People, to lead by example and make a stand, to ensure the continuity of our culture. To be able to take this responsibility that has been given to us since birth, we the young, require guidance and support from our Elders. There are leaders, and there are supporters, each are equally important and are vital to reaching our pinnacle.

People say 'don't dwell in the past'. However, the past constitutes who we are today. How can you go forward when you don't know where you have been? You can learn from the past to better the future. Learn from your mistakes.

I remember one of my uncles saying that when a rock is thrown into a pond, there are ripple effects that follow after. The impact was the Stolen Generations, assimilation, dispossession, massacres, and the removal of our Old People's remains. The ripple effects are what we continue to see today, for example, oppression, degradation, humiliation, unemployment, poor health, inverted racism and the loss of language. Although we as the Aboriginal people have been subject to these horrific wrong doings of Australia's shameful and mostly unspoken past, we are still asking for reconciliation.

Kaysha Taylor (2007) began her email story by tracing her ties to her father, a Nyoongar man from Perth in Western Australia and her mother, a Bungarla woman from the Eyre Peninsula of South Australia and noted that her bloodline ran through the Ngarrindjeri, Narungga and Kaurna groups of South Australia. When Kaysha talks of her family she is candid. Her parents had a hard life. The lives of several of her family were deeply scarred by alcohol and drugs, other family members became respected role models. She speaks with enormous respect of her mother, sister and brother. Of her childhood, Kaysha Taylor (2007) wrote: I grew up surrounded by cousins and

 constantly with my parents and grandparent. I remember Nanna would often tell stories about her growing up on the missions and how hard it was to be accepted by what she would call the 'white community'. She was a hard working woman but always went home thinking that all her work went to waste and was viewed as nothing, simply because she was

Indigenous. My grandmother would often tell us stories of the Dreamtime and taught us lessons that were taught through stories. These stories are so important to me because I dream that one day I can tell my stories to my children and guide them in the right path. Having the knowledge from your family and Elders is so important but it seems that the new generation are ignoring this knowledge when it is probably the most important within the Aboriginal cultures. These stories have been passed on from generation to generation.

Many of my relations grew up under the surveillance of white people. They were treated like criminals and lived their lives where discrimination was a part of their everyday life. Today they tell my generation to never give in to racism or to discrimination. My grandmother would tell me how important education is. She would tell me that she wasn't allowed to go to high school because she was Aboriginal. She was stripped of the rights to be who she wanted to be so today my Elders always tell me to seize opportunities as soon as I am given them.

A lot of Aboriginal children of my generation don't have the same respect for the land as our Elders do. I have been told numerous times that I should respect those who are around me, those being either humans or animals. I was told the Dreaming of creations and the Dreamings of how we came to be and these stories should forever be passed down generation to generation.

Role models

Over and over again the young women spoke of strong women in their lives who were role models for them and the older women recalled women who had mentored and guided them. Aunty Ellen Trevorrow paid tribute to her sisters-in-law, Aunty Alice Abdulla and Aunty Rita Lindsay. She recalled their importance to her in her younger days and said how happy she was they had returned to live nearby. Alice was always a role model for me. I've always looked up to them, to her and Bill. One night, this is back when I was pregnant with my first child, Tom and me were hitch-hiking out of Meningie. We were going to live with his two sisters, with Alice and Rita. But we only got out there to where those pine trees are, about three miles out. No-one would give us a lift. So we slept under the pine trees. It was really cold. We came home the next day. We were meant to be here. Then they came home. When they moved back, it was so lovely. It's beautiful having them all back.

Edie Carter looked around the room and said: We have heaps of role models, here, everywhere. Mine would be Aunty Ellen and Uncle Laurie Rankine. When did we become role models? asked Aunty Eileen McHughes, half in jest.

Kaysha Taylor (2007) wrote at length of the importance of her mother as a role model, of her gratitude to her family for their support and her own ambition to be a role model in the community: I was ten when my mother took on responsibility of her youngest brother's children and so my four cousins aged five months to six years became part of our family. As a single parent still caring for my sister and I, she took on these younger children: two were still in nappies and one not being able to walk. At first it was a shock but very inspirational. It was then that my mother opened my eyes as to who she really was. She is my role model and mentor, a strong Aboriginal woman.

My sister is probably my best friend. We've had our fights but we both know how much we lose when not being with each other. Because of my own achievements she has sacrificed a lot just to make sure I have the time to follow my dreams. And I am forever grateful.

I have always known how I wanted to end up. Since primary school I've wanted to better myself and be a leading role model in my community. I worked the hardest I could at high school and with doing that I was awarded a scholarship and the chance to travel to America on a student exchange program with Rotary. Those twelve months were amazing and I learnt a lot. My mother sacrificed a lot for me to have that opportunity so I strived for the best when I returned. The first month I got back into Australia I applied at the University of Adelaide and was accepted into law. I got a part time job working as an Aboriginal education worker supporting Indigenous students at a nearby primary school. Youth work has been a passion since high school. The thrill of seeing an Aboriginal child succeed is precious. What's most precious about it is that you see how much their perspective of life changes when giving them the opportunity to follow their dreams.

Eunice Aston runs workshops that encourage young women to shine. Strong women. We all know women are the backbone of family and we're so focussed on family and our work in the community, that we work, work, work and Ngarrindjeri women in particular, because that's my experience, we're watching our grannies and nieces and nephews and we forget to look after ourselves. As she says this, Eunice Aston swoops her granny up in her arms and kisses her. When the men are away, we need to remember that we can take care of things and we always were able to do that. I see young girls becoming dependent on men and forgetting that we are fearless. I was about three or four and my grandmother was telling me about our women and their strength and she'd chuck the men out when they brought alcohol into the house. So she was telling stories and practicing what she was preaching. She was a good role model. I was lucky that way, on both sides, I had a strong role model. Strong and fearless. Later in the evening, we talked about strong women and Warrior Women. The women smiled and nodded sagely.

Women's well-being

When Ngarrindjeri *miminar* gather, there is often talk of strong women and the Warrior Woman tradition. In the 19th century, the Rev. George Taplin recorded the Seven Sisters as one of the deceased warriors who have gone to heaven (Taplin 1873:18; Bell 1998:581). The story of the Seven Sisters (see Chapter Two) includes the ordeals they endure in their passage from girlhood to womanhood. These are strong, resolute women (Unaipon 1925:42-3).

Today Ngarrindjeri *miminar* say: We want to stand strong, stand together. We want to take an active role by learning self-defence for women, running women's neighbourhood watch programs. Other women spoke of the ways in which they can help their daughters when there is domestic violence. "Come home," I told her. "That's no way for you to live, or your children." And she did come back. That's what a mother can advise. And, it's not just the physical violence, there's the verbal abuse too, a number of younger women said. There needs to be a bigger focus on verbal violence and its effects; a focus on the use of a 'Respect Language' and inclusion of 'Respect Behaviour'. If we can identify the abuse caused by disrespectful language and behaviours towards each other, we can do something about it.

At the October 2007 Ngarrindjeri *Miminar* Gathering held at Camp Coorong, Aunty Eunice Aston conducted a women's leadership workshop with goals including: bringing Elders and young women together so they could share stories and learn from each other; promoting awareness of Aboriginal women's social justice issues; encouraging the participation of young Aboriginal women in community meetings; improving the self-esteem, health and well-being of Aboriginal women.

Aunty Eunice Aston has a way of making things real when she speaks. She draws on her own life and invites others to share their concerns. My whole life is family, culture and heritage. I have twenty grannies, well eighteen really, there's twins still on the way: five each from my three eldest, three from my step-daughter. All told I have ten children, five of my own, two step-children and three nephews. Family: I'm a daughter, a sister, cousin, and niece. I'm a wife, mother and grandmother. That's my life.

At the moment, I'm assessing what I'm doing. Looking back and looking forward. Thinking where do I want to be in ten years? That will include continuing my education to become a registered nurse.

Eunice Aston, Camp Coorong, June 24, 2007

Photograph: Annie Vanderwyk

Today I'm running the Women's Leadership program, putting the young ones together with the old ones. I tell them, "Take serious issues, work with them, make them part of us and come together as women." And I tell them, "We'll let you know when it's time. You'll know when you're tapped." I don't want to see our young girls assuming leadership roles before they're ready. I don't want young girls getting burnt out, like me, at 48. When Aunty Veronica and Aunty Maggie tapped me, I wasn't sure I was ready, but they tapped me and I knew I was being told I was ready and I had to assume that responsibility. I take it really serious when I'm elected by people to do a job, since we went to Sydney with Aunty Dot, Aunty Veronica, Aunty Gracie and Aunty Hazel, where I was authorised to speak.

At the moment I'm the State Rural Representative for the Women's Gathering. The Office of Women here in South Australia has a yearly gathering and delegates are elected for the rural sector. From that I became the National Delegate for SA and we take our views from the local level to Ministerial Council.

The issues are pressing. Substance abuse (alcohol and other drugs) was identified as one cause of violence and family breakdown. Middle age and older women bear the burden of addicted teenage daughters with babies and sons looking for drug money. In the old days socially disruptive individuals were ostracised or banished. Today trouble-makers and abusers are often hidden behind closed doors. No longer can older wiser relatives intervene, caution, help to ease tension by consoling a crying child, or by offering a refuge for a fearful wife. Nuclear families become the social unit where aberrant behaviours are witnessed.

Of drugs Aunty Eunice Aston recalls: First alcohol was whipping our families and then about 30 years ago *yarndi* [cannabis] came in and it practically incapacitated the men. They didn't want to do anything. But hard drugs, that's about the last fifteen years. I see mothers crying. I see ODs and suicides. It's a lost generation, from about their late 30s down.

Suggested solutions included demanding more rehabilitation programs, ones that are culturally appropriate, safe houses for women and children, 24-hour support services, responsive police. We want the police to come when we ask for help. We don't want them hanging around waiting for trouble. Edie Carter said: Let the kids tell their stories in their own way. It might be rap, a poem, whatever. Let them tell about what they're facing. And let them hear from the Elders, know what they're feeling. Use respect for the Elders. We grew up with that we have to use it before it is too late. Start now. Get onto them, before they lose it.

Then there are the problems around sex and sexuality. Aunty Eunice Aston: Really young girls are getting pregnant, really they're raped because they wake up and don't know what has happened and are too shamed to do anything. I see the American influence on Aboriginal culture. I see our culture could slip away. It's distressing.

Georgie Trevorrow (2007) wrote: The younger generation having babies (children having children), that makes me sad. A lot of the young girls who are out there having sex and they don't think about contraception and then it's too late, they're either pregnant or they'll catch STI (sexual transmitted infections), then of course they leave it too late because they are ashamed of what they have done, and sometimes it makes things worse.

In terms of health and well-being, Ngarrindjeri *miminar* sought a total package that would include access to reliable and culturally appropriate medical information, classes in nutrition for Aboriginal people, birth control, safe sex, parenting skills, respite care. They noted the lack of transportation for medical care for Elders, families and youth; more help on education and health and STIs, and parenting classes, especially for younger mums.

When discussion turned to sex-education the women had a number of things to say.

Q. At what age should children be taught about 'safe sex'?

A. It depends on how mature they are. There's a limit on what they can ask. They know about it. They listen to their peer group talk about videos.

I took my granddaughter out of the classes. She was too young to be hearing those things. They need accurate information that is age appropriate.

I'd rather they know right and wrong than have friends telling them made up things.

You've got to be careful with what you say to kids and in front of kids.

Q. Who should tell young women about sex?

A. They should come to the mother.

It wasn't my mother who told me.

Parents need awareness of what kids know through videos and their peer group.

We want parents to be open-minded and not to push the kids away. If parents are aware they'll ask some kids. They're too shame to ask. Parents need to be approachable.

Younger kids are hanging out with older kids. They hear talk. There is pressure.

They need to hang out with their own age. We need to hear what they're saying.

Youth workers need to listen and tell parents they need to talk to their children.

How can young girls value themselves when there are so many demeaning images? When they are subject to double standards? Aunty Eileen McHughes sighed and said, I'm glad I'm just a grandmother.

Rita Lindsay Jr (2007) wrote: The justice system desperately needs to be changed so that offenders are sentenced to the full extent of the law. Today, we are seeing too many cases where perpetrators are not receiving their rightful punishment for the crimes that they have committed and are instead being handed lesser charges, for example, manslaughter instead of murder, particularly in domestic violence cases. Advertisements are saying 'To domestic violence, Australia says no' but the law is saying something else. Why have a law, when it cannot be enforced where necessary.

The Ngarrindjeri Nation is investing in its young people by widening their horizons. Aunty Ellen Trevorrow spoke about her son Luke and his work experience in Adelaide when he was in Year 11. He saw the homeless and it changed his life. He came back and told us about it. We need to move them. Now we have three in Melbourne at the Initiatives of Change program,[22] and when they come back, they'll tell the others.

Rita Lindsay Jr (2007) wrote of her experience: On the 28th of June to the 8th of July 2007, I attended the Life Matters course at Armagh, Melbourne. The course gave me an opportunity to interact with a diverse range of nationalities as there were fifteen representatives from eleven countries. The course was both an educational and enjoyable experience. The knowledge that I obtained from this course will enable me as a young Ngarrindjeri woman to influence and encourage the younger generation to reconnect with their culture for the ultimate goal of establishing a stronger connection to country through music, traditional dance, arts and crafts.

Whilst attending the Life Matters course I was able to share my culture through traditional Ngarrindjeri dance, weaving and feather flowers. My persistence and determination to pass on my knowledge to the younger generations and to learn from my Elders in preparation of becoming a leader raised curiosity. The participants at the Life Matters course were fascinated with the Ngarrindjeri traditions and our strong connection to the land, waters and our *ngatji* [totems].

The Life Matters course taught individuals to establish a connection to something, not materialistic but to a higher power, religion: a source that has the power to provide you with the strength to remain strong, both mentally and physically. The individuals at the Life Matters course could see that we had already established a connection, we had learned from young through having respect for the land, all living things and for ourselves and others. However, by attending this course I developed a stronger sense of independence, enhanced my knowledge and awareness of the issues that we are faced with worldwide. I believe that the only way to confront these issues is to work in collaboration, which can be reached through the process of reconciliation. The question that I ask is 'Why is it so hard for non-Aboriginals and Aboriginals to work together?'

The course was enjoyable as there was no hierarchical order and I felt that I did not have to contend with any racist attitudes. It was evident that reconciliation was achievable at Armagh.

The Life Matters Coordinator, John Mills, wrote to Mrs Ellen Trevorrow on July 12, 2007: "It was a joy to have Rita, Julie [Carter] and Bessie [Rigney] with us for the Life Matters Course. They contributed so much in their own distinctive ways. Everyone was so appreciative of the contribution and we hope they will return at some stage to help us with future courses."

The tightness of the stitches is like the closeness of the family, said Aunty Dodo using weaving as a metaphor for family. Powerful forces have threatened and continue to threaten the fabric of families: Stolen Generations of children and Old People, racism and ignorance. But the Ngarrindjeri have not given up. They have petitioned governments, negotiated agreements and led by example. One innovation has been the incorporation of a number of existing organisations to form the Ngarrindjeri Regional Authority.

Caring for the Nation

> The weaving is about our history, all the Ngarrindjeri past.
> As we weave from the centre out, we weave the Ngarrindjeri world,
> like our *miwi*. It is not cut into little boxes.
>
> *Daisy Rankine (Bell 1998:542)*

> We need to be valued. Women need to be valued. Men need to be valued.
> We need a centre for culture, for research, for men, women and children.
> We need employment, self-governance. We need to build self-esteem,
> confidence and pride in ourselves. Instead of our *miwi* grieving, it will rejoice
> and we can return to being a happy nation again.
>
> *Aunty Eileen McHughes (2007)*

Ngarrindjeri Regional Authority

At the first of our workshops in June 2007, we took up the issue of Ngarrindjeri *miminar's* roles and responsibilities as members of the Ngarrindjeri Nation. The women began with the Ngarrindjeri Regional Authority Inc. (NRA), a new body that brought together the leaders of existing Ngarrindjeri committees into one structure. They explored four key issues:

- What are our needs?
- What do we want to address our needs?
- Where are we going?
- What does the future hold for us, our children, our grandchildren, our young women?

All women present wanted more involvement in governance, meetings, policy formation, decision-making, and to be taken seriously on a range of issues. The struggle to protect women's sacred places on *Kumarangk* drove home the importance of bringing women into decisions about heritage and development. Through their work with their menfolk on the CSIRO project, the women had further opportunities to speak on matters of resource management and caring for country.[23] So where did women fit within the NRA?

The idea behind the NRA was to work towards the vision of the Ngarrindjeri Nation set out in the *Yarluwar-Ruwe Plan – Sea Country Plan* (Ngarrindjeri Tendi *et al* 2006). The Ngarrindjeri Governance Working Party, chaired by Uncle George Trevorrow and comprising representatives of the Ngarrindjeri Lands and Progress Association; the Ngarrindjeri Tendi; Ngarrindjeri Native Title Management Committee; Ngarrindjeri Heritage Committee; Kalparrin Community Council Inc.; Lower Murray Nungas Club; Tangglun Piltengi Yunti Aboriginal Corporation; Mannum Aboriginal Community Association Inc.; and Fleurieu Aboriginal Progress Association Inc. met over a period of

Day Two: Ngarrindjeri *miminar* meet to discuss the Ngarrindjeri Regional Authority, Camp Coorong, June 24, 2007

Back row: Vicki Hartman, Georgie Trevorrow, Thelma Smart, Alice Abdulla, Anne McMahon, Eileen McHughes, Hilda Day, Eunice Aston, Rita Lindsay Sr, Rita Lindsay Jr, Margaret Dodd, Julie Carter, Noreen Kartinyeri, Audrey Lindsay, Annie Vanderwyk, Helen Jackson, Bessie Rigney.

Front row: Georgina Trevorrow, holding Georgia Trevorrow, Shirley Trevorrow, Dorothy Kartinyeri holding Cheyeanne Carter, Latoya Love with Edie Carter, Donna Kartinyeri holding Phoebe Kartinyeri, Ellen Trevorrow.

Photograph: Annie Vanderwyk

eighteen months, mostly at Murray Bridge. They sought a coordinated approach in dealing with government agencies, such as Natural Resources Management. With the demise of the Aboriginal and Torres Strait Islander Commission (ATSIC), the demand on the Ngarrindjeri leadership by a range of government bureaucracies has been overwhelming. Consultants, each seeking information regarding specific projects,

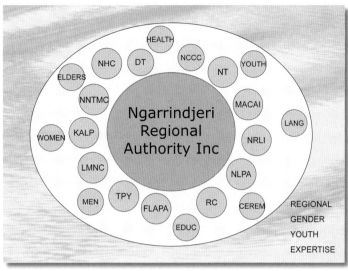

The Ngarrindjeri Regional Authority: The Circle of Ngarrindjeri Governance

come and go but contribute little to the community priorities that the Ngarrindjeri have been articulating. The dangers of fragmentation are real. The leadership hoped the NRA would be a forum in which Ngarrindjeri could plan, forge policy, and speak with one voice on matters of Native Title, Heritage issues, economic development, service delivery and social issues. As an incorporated body, the NRA could hold property, run businesses, seek funds, commission research, protect intellectual property rights and cultural knowledge. Further, the NRA would make it possible for the Ngarrindjeri to negotiate Nation to Nation on the international stage, a process already underway with reference to the Umatilla of Portland, Oregon, USA.[24]

The Rules of the Ngarrindjeri Regional Authority Inc., state that the Objects are:

6.1 The Association is established and will be maintained for charitable purposes as the Committee may from time to time determine concerning Ngarrindjeri People by establishing and maintaining suitable and appropriate services, facilities, enterprises, property, infrastructure and

legend for abbreviations

cerem = ceremony;

educ = education;

lang = language

NCCC Ngarrindjeri Caring for Country Centre

NHC Ngarrindjeri Heritage Committee

NNTMC Ngarrindjeri Native Title Management Committee

NRLI Ngarrindjeri Research and Learning Institute

NT Ngarrindjeri Tendi

LMNC Lower Murray Nungas Club

NLPA Ngarrindjeri Land and Progress Association

KALP Kalparrin Community Council Inc

TPY Tangglun Piltengi Yunti Aboriginal Corporation

RC Raukkan Council

MACAI Mannum Aboriginal Community Association Inc

DT Dapung Talkinyeri

FLAPA Fleurieu Aboriginal Progress Association Inc

There are seats for other Ngarrindjeri organisations.

other similar benefits which collectively benefit of Ngarrindjeri People or any of their funds, trusts, authorities, or institutions whose ordinary income and statutory income is exempt from income tax under Division 50 of Part 2-15 of the *Income Tax Assessment Act 1997.*

6.2 Subject to and without limiting the generality of clause 6.1, the purpose of the Association is to:

6.2.1. promote the welfare of the Ngarrindjeri People;

6.2.2. assist the Ngarrindjeri People to protect areas of special significance to them in accordance with tradition and custom;

6.2.3 advance the health and welfare of the Ngarrindjeri People;

6.2.4. improve and increase the economic opportunities of the Ngarrindjeri People with a view to alleviating poverty and promoting other charitable purposes;

6.2.5 facilitate and assist the Ngarrindjeri People in community projects and social welfare programs benefiting Aboriginal people;

6.2.6. to unite the Ngarrindjeri People seeking to have their Native Title rights and interests recognised in respect of lands which comprise or form part of Ngarrindjeri Lands including pursuing the Native Title Application;

6.2.7. to initiate legal proceedings or seek any administrative remedies, if appropriate, to protect, preserve and prevent interference with places of historical, social, cultural and spiritual significance for the Ngarrindjeri People, as well as for the purposes of protecting and preserving the Native Title rights and interests of the Ngarrindjeri People;

6.2.8. to conduct research and gather information necessary for the assertion of traditional rights and interests over Ngarrindjeri Lands including Native Title rights and interests;

6.2.9. to enter into agreements with other entities, including, but not limited to, other Aboriginal Peoples and Aboriginal Associations, the Commonwealth or State Governments, private corporations and individuals, in relation to land, cultural knowledge, heritage, or any other rights or interests connected or associated with the Ngarrindjeri People;

6.2.10. to manage land of traditional or cultural significance to the Ngarrindjeri People and to hold any interest in such land as trustee or otherwise for the Ngarrindjeri People;

6.2.11. to act as the trustee under any trust established for the benefit of the Ngarrindjeri People;

6.2.12. to protect the intellectual property rights of the Ngarrindjeri People, including but not limited to:

> 6.2.12.1. traditions, observances, customs and beliefs;
>
> 6.2.12.2. songs, music, dances, stories, ceremonies, symbols, narratives and designs;
>
> 6.2.12.3. languages;
>
> 6.2.12.4. spiritual knowledge;
>
> 6.2.12.5. traditional economies and resources management;
>
> 6.2.12.6. scientific, spatial, agricultural, technical, biological and ecological knowledge; and includes documentation or other forms of media arising there from including but not limited to archives, films, photographs, videotape or audiotape.

A place was designated within the NRA for representation of women's concerns. We are serious about caring for our children and grandchildren. We care about the future. This is how Georgie Trevorrow, Georgina Trevorrow, Aunty Eileen McHughes, Aunty Vicki Hartman and Aunty Shirley Trevorrow spoke of their well-being as Ngarrindjeri women. Other women added:

Women need to have an equal voice.

Women's well-being is a vital part of the well-being of the Ngarrindjeri Nation.

We need people to listen when we speak, to acknowledge what we say. No tokenism.

Shared responsibility for family and country and governance.

We need to be proud people.

All the women present agreed they needed representation on the NRA. If NRA is our peak body, women need representation. We need access to information and time to develop understanding of the matters addressed by the NRA, said Aunty Eileen McHughes. There was clear agreement that each major committee needed a Women's Officer and, at the level of the NRA, there needed to be a space for a Women's Portfolio. The officers on each committee would then be responsible for communicating to members of their group and also reporting to the Women's Portfolio. In setting up committees and meeting times, they asked that there be consideration of family needs, transportation and location.

We need better communications, said Aunty Thelma Smart, Aunty Helen Jackson and Donna Kartinyeri. If the NRA is going to work for us, we need access to Elders, better communication through newsletters, websites, emails, and to be present at meetings or have someone who could report back to us from meetings. Again they stressed that meeting schedules need to take account of their needs as mothers and to recognise that not all have access to vehicles or hold a driver's licence. Getting information out to members of the Ngarrindjeri Nation is a difficult task. Currently much information is spread by word of mouth but because Ngarrindjeri live in far-flung communities, not everyone is well-informed. Attention needs to be given to how committee members can keep their constituents informed of committee business. Constituents need ways through which they can communicate their concerns to their representatives. One proposal is to establish a regional network with sophisticated wireless broadband technology that would link communities across Ngarrindjeri country (see Ngarrindjeri Regional Authority 2008).

The *Tendi*

The concept of a Regional Authority that brings a number of interests and groups within its ambit has its roots in traditional Ngarrindjeri law with the institution known as the *Tendi* and 'chiefs' known as *Rupelli*. Early observers of Ngarrindjeri life such as The Rev. George Taplin whose 1859–79 journals record daily comings and goings at the Point McLeay mission describe the *Tendi* as the Council of Elders of the tribe consisting of leaders of the tribe and states that every clan has a chief, called a *Rupelli* (or landowner) (Taplin 1879:35). "Justice," Taplin (1879:36) writes, "is administered by the *tendi* in accordance with the customs handed down by tradition in the tribe". In his journals, Taplin (1859:9/11) describes the Ngarrindjeri (Narrinyeri) as "a powerful confederacy". Of the governance structure of the people of the Lower Murray, the Berndts write they "were unique in Aboriginal Australia: they had not only an institutionalized clan leadership but also a formalized council or court" which the Berndts call *yanarumi* (Berndt *et al* 1993:58).

Knowledge of the *Tendi* system has been passed down by Ngarrindjeri Elders and, following a meeting of Ngarrindjeri leaders at Tailem Bend in 1992, the institution was formally reinvigorated. At that meeting, Nanna Laura Kartinyeri, granddaughter of 'Queen Louisa', was made a life-time member of the *Tendi* and she authorised the renewed activity of the *Tendi*. After considerable discussion regarding membership, Nanna Laura, with due regard for changes that had occurred in Ngarrindjeri society, declared that traditional initiation was no longer a requirement for membership. The *Tendi* continues to function as a Ngarrindjeri institution and is the body to whom matters of tradition may be referred. The nature of the matters has expanded because the nature of life in the region has changed, but the *Tendi* remains a central part the governance structure of the nation. George Trevorrow was elected *Rupelli* in accordance with Ngarrindjeri law and the current Ngarrindjeri *Tendi* is one of the organisations represented within the NRA.

The historic record contains valuable information about the election of women to leadership roles, called 'Queen' (in the language of the day). The *Register*, May 11, 1927 carried an article: 'A dusky ruler' written by 'E.S.A.' A photocopy of the news clipping is displayed at the entrance to the museum at Camp Coorong.

The article presents the record of a chat with Granny Ethel Wympie Watson from Kingston in which she recalls the early days and the ritual that marked her out as a leader of her people. My Aunt Catherine told me that when she was made Queen, there was big Doings. Days of dancing, hunting, and making feast, and all our wurlies full of our people. Then she wore some native beads, and the chief one of the tribe made long talk, and there was much corroboree. So she became the head of us all. But when I was made Queen, it was not so big a time. We went away back into the bush, and there were night fires and corroborees, and I wore the beads, too. The term 'Queen' may be a colonial artefact, but the tradition

The Register, May 11, 1927 with photograph of Queen Ethel wearing the ceremonial beads

of acknowledging particular women as important and their matrilineal kin bestowing honours upon them is not.

According to the ethnographic record, women had a role in the clan-based *Tendi* and appeared as witnesses in the over-arching *Tendi* (Berndt *et al* 1993:65ff). Today, the issues facing the Ngarrindjeri Nation extend beyond those the *Tendi* addressed in the nineteenth century. Women are clear that they have a role in the NRA and that it is consistent with their responsibilities as Ngarrindjeri *miminar* for their families and for their country. In their view, a portfolio for Women's Affairs with women's representatives on each of the committees reporting to that person would ensure that the various perspectives of women on matters of culture, employment, health, education, housing, and nurturing of family members would be heard. Aunty Eileen already serves on a number of committees – Lower Murray Nungas Club, Elders Committee, Aboriginal Housing Management Committee, Aboriginal Child Care and more – and sits on the NRA. She has no doubts that Ngarrindjeri *miminar* have an important role to play in the future of the Nation.

We have never ceded nor sold our lands

On December 17, 2003, Uncle George Trevorrow, Uncle Matt Rigney, Uncle Tom Trevorrow and Aunty Ellen Trevorrow presented the 'Proclamation of Ngarrindjeri Dominium' to the then South Australian Governor, Marjorie Jackson-Nelson. As a mark of respect and in due keeping with the solemnity of the occasion, Aunty Ellen had woven a sister basket in which the Proclamation was placed for presentation. The document stated: "The Ngarrindjeri have always **occupied** the traditional lands of the Ngarrindjeri Nation and Ngarrindjeri have never **ceded** nor sold our lands and waters" (emphasis in original).

In their Proclamation the Ngarrindjeri called upon the South Australian government to address this undertaking and to:

> **ONE:**
> **Enter a Social Contract with the Ngarrindjeri to inscribe the mutual recognition of our dominium as between the Ngarrindjeri Nation and the Crown within South Australia;** <u>and</u>
> **TWO:**
> **Present Parliament with a Bill for a Ngarrindjeri treaty** to be enacted by indenture, which secures the Dominium of our Ngarrindjeri lands and waters to the perpetual inheritance of the Ngarrindjeri Nation, and which enshrines a Bill of Rights for the advancement of the human rights of all South Australians, and the particular maintenance of the Ngarrindjeri heritage in perpetuity (emphasis in original).

Receipt of the Proclamation was acknowledged but there has been no action on the idea of a social contract. There have, however, been promising acknowledgements of the need to attend to the matter of the Letters Patent of 1836.

The Ngarrindjeri Proclamation sets out a history that the Ngarrindjeri are keen to share concerning the legal history of the establishment of South

Australia and the nature of the promises made to the original inhabitants (see Appendix Two). They point to an important provision contained within the Letters Patent of 1836 issued to Governor Hindmarsh in London by the Crown of the United Kingdom of Great Britain.

The delegation at the gates of Government House: Elders Tom Trevorrow, Ellen Trevorrow, Matthew Rigney and George Trevorrow

Photograph: Ngarrindjeri Heritage Committee Inc.

> PROVIDED ALWAYS that nothing in those Letters Patent contained shall affect or be construed to affect the rights of any Aboriginal Natives of the said Province to the actual occupation or enjoyment in their own Persons or in Persons of their Descendants of any lands therein now actually occupied or enjoyed by such Natives.[25]

On December 28, 2006, at the Old Gum Tree, Glenelg, South Australia, at the Proclamation Day ceremony that commemorates the establishment of the Province of South Australia, The Honorable Jay Weatherill MP, Minister for Aboriginal Affairs and Reconciliation said:

> Today it is important to remember that we failed to keep our promise to Aboriginal People … The Letters Patent establishing South Australia expressly provide for the rights of Aboriginal People … I believe we must recommit ourselves to the promise made to Aboriginal South Australians at this place 170 years ago.[26]

On Proclamation Day, December 28, 2007 at the city of Holdfast Bay, His Excellency Rear Admiral Kevin Scarce, Governor of South Australia, stated:

> There can be no doubt that the lives and future of the indigenous people of South Australia were irrevocably changed in 1836. Despite the intent to protect the native population that is expressed in the Proclamation, there can be no dispute that these aspirations were not

always realised. The well-intentioned desire to promote (and I quote) their advancement in civilisation has proved to be a mixed blessing.

Whilst acknowledging the mistakes of the past, we must confront the reality that the solutions lie in the present and in the future. It is important for the well-being of our whole society that the interests of our indigenous citizens are not only protected but also advanced, in ways that reflect their aspirations.

I know of no easy solution. Dialogue, good will and compromise will be required in order to successfully address this national challenge.[27]

Since the Proclamation of 1836, the Ngarrindjeri have made a number of calls for honourable, just, equitable and democratic outcomes. They have petitioned and proclaimed. They have applied and appealed. In short they have used the democratic process and they have done so according to their protocols. The process has been one of seeking recognition and agreement-making in relation to their future well-being (Rigney *et al* in press).

At the June 2007 workshop, the women reflected on the existence of the Letters Patent and the need for a treaty.

Q. What do these words mean to us today? If we were negotiating a treaty today, what would we women ask for?

A.
- We want more *kungun* (listening) and more *yunnan* (talking).
- Respect for our families.
- Respect for our laws.
- Respect for culture, our land and our waters and the air we breathe.
- Independence of life.

If Ngarrindjeri dominion over our lands were to be recognised, we would seek
- Compensation for lands appropriated;
- Crown Land. Give that to us, for us as a form of compensation for your error;
- A compensation package with adequate resources for
  - o Repatriation
  - o Cultural awareness programs for non-Ngarrindjeri
  - o Stolen Generations;
- Non-Indigenous people would need to get permission to live on and use Ngarrindjeri land;
- Non-Indigenous people would have to consult with the Traditional Owners of the land about matters concerning their *ruwi;*

- Ngarrindjeri as Sovereign Peoples would have the right to deport undesirables and the right to choose what boat people were to be accepted to our land;
- Ngarrindjeri would require access to all government resources and documents concerning their lives.

Diane asked how researchers who work with the Ngarrindjeri would fare under such a regime and was told with the enormous good humour that characterised this part of the workshop: Ngarrindjeri would issue permits and exemption cards to enter special places for non-Ngarrindjeri.

The NRA is keeping the issue of the Letters Patent on their agenda and Shaun Berg of Hunt and Hunt, lawyer for the Ngarrindjeri, has been collating relevant materials and is preparing an edited collection of legal commentary, opinion and research on the experience of Indigenous peoples at home and abroad (see also Rigney *et al* in press).

Looking ahead

A typical list of issues the NRA should address included:

- Culture
- Heritage
- Health and well-being
- Craftworks
- Communication
- Support groups
- Better housing
- Youth
- Economic development
- Education and training

A typical assessment of the current situation was: Not good at the moment. We need all of the above.

Rita Lindsay Jr (2007) wrote of her vision for the Ngarrindjeri Nation: I believe that the Ngarrindjeri Nation is headed in a new direction. The establishment of the Ngarrindjeri Regional Authority will bring about the organisation and unification of the *Laklinyerar* [Clans]. The Ngarrindjeri Regional Authority will offer an opportunity for our people to display independence as a nation. The NRA is a seed, the beginning; it is a foundation for the future generations to come. For a nation to be successful, the people must work in collaboration. For any goal to be successful, there needs to be commitment, dedication, hard work, faith, hope, focus and knowledge. These aspects would be some of the pillars of strength that would support our path to achieve our goals. It is time for us to be self-reliant. What will the day be like when we will no longer require financial assistance from the Government? Every time they cut our funding we feel the impact, we are crippled as a business.

We will be able to create employment, establish Independence as a people and set an example for all Aboriginal people. Our culture, language, people, traditions will have once again demonstrated that even though we were subject to the wrong doings of the past, we have still been able to withstand the force of the western world.

Through their organisations, the newly established NRA, and the agreements that structure their interactions with outside agencies, the Ngarrindjeri are generating a sound foundation for their Nation, one where they can begin to set the priorities. There are high hopes that the NRA will provide the framework for the Ngarrindjeri Nation to move forward with its plans. In their announcement 'A significant Day for Ngarrindjeri People', the NRA stated: [28]

It is the view of the Ngarrindjeri Regional Authority that through working together under this new arrangement and building partnerships and agreement making with all levels of Government and business that Ngarrindjeri People will gain a stronger position in addressing poverty, unemployment, disadvantage, boredom, drug and alcohol abuse. We want to work together to create a better lifestyle for our children's future through employment, good schooling and higher education opportunities. We plan to begin this new approach to partnership, policy and planning through the work of the new Ngarrindjeri Regional Authority. Our first focus is the development of Ngarrindjeri Caring for Country program that combines our culture heritage and beliefs with education and economic development. We believe that our lands and waters must be healthy before the Ngarrindjeri people can be strong and healthy.

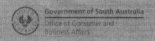

Government of South Australia
Office of Consumer and
Business Affairs

SOUTH AUSTRALIA

Associations Incorporation Act 1985
Section 20(1)

Incorporation Number: **A39455**

Certificate of Incorporation

This is to certify that

NGARRINDJERI REGIONAL AUTHORITY INCORPORATED

is, on and from the third day of May 2007
incorporated under the Associations Incorporation Act 1985.

Given under the seal of the Corporate Affairs Commission at Adelaide on this
third day of May 2007

Commissioner for Corporate Affairs

Certificate of Incorporation of the
Ngarrindjeri Regional Authority, 2007

Economic Development[29]

Chapter 5

> Some of them, when they left Raukkan [the mission], or wherever they were, would bring their weaving. They would carry whatever they were making. And it didn't come to me until my sister Leila said, You think about it. They'd tell the White Christians they were coming away to pick rushes, and to do more weaving. They'd be gone for a few days. Mum would come with her grandmother. While they were here doing the women's business, which the White Christians didn't know about, they would also take in a bit of trading. So, you see, the women's business was always taken care of but no-one knew what was going on. All they knew was that the women had gone away from there to do some weaving, pick more rushes, and the only ones to know about it were the ones that they knew that were trusted. Goolwa was a trading place. They told Taplin [Rev George Taplin at Raukkan 1859–79] they were getting rushes and that they were trading, all of which was true.
>
> *Aunty Veronica Brodie (Bell 1998:86–7)*

Working with the NRA

Mission rules and regulations placed an enormous burden on Ngarrindjeri *miminar*. Mission expectations of 'good women' did not include participating in ceremonies, but it did include productive labour. As Aunty Veronica tells us, during their days off the mission the women could enjoy time in their country, attend to women's business and spend time together. They had found a way to be 'good women' according to missionary precepts and 'women of worth' according to their own. Similarly in Aunty Ellen Trevorrow's story of her Nanna Brown's trips up and down the river when she was "making trade…for us", we hear of how women were caring for country while engaging in economic activities. How to survive in these modern times demands clever thinking about economic development. That guidance is in the stories. In thinking about a contemporary issue such as 'economic development', Ngarrindjeri *miminar* can draw on a heritage, one in which the principles of sustainable economic development are embedded in the wider cultural concerns of well-being, caring for country, caring for family and survival. Ngarrindjeri *miminar* know that economic development is not a separate issue but a continuation of Ngarrindjeri practice where the world of *ngatji*, story, the Old People and current generations are interwoven.

One of the stated goals of the NRA (6.2.4) is to "develop projects that will improve and increase the economic opportunities of the Ngarrindjeri Nation with a view to alleviating poverty and promoting other charitable purposes". Here is what the women said:

We want equal recognition of our role in the community and governance of the Nation through business development.

We want to become self-sufficient, set our own priorities. We are tired of being told what is good for us by people who don't know us.

Partnerships with state, national and international tourism enterprises will help us create stronger relationships within family and *laklinyerar* [clan groups] for caring for country and networking within the groups.

All the women's proposals began with the proposition that the Ngarrindjeri Nation needs to own the land on which they can develop their enterprises. Only then would they be able to make decisions and follow through according to their priorities. The NRA would be the body to which women could bring their plans for the development of various programs. It may be possible to plan various facilities in conjunction with other Ngarrindjeri property developments. The NRA would play a critical role in facilitating equitable business partnerships with local builders and land developers which would mean quicker realisation of these projects that would benefit the whole community.

Georgie Trevorrow, Georgina Trevorrow, Aunty Eileen McHughes, Aunty Vicki Hartman and Aunty Shirley Trevorrow stated that business development could be seen as a vehicle to create employment while caring for country. Others recognised that the establishment of private businesses and Ngarrindjeri Nation partnerships would further the equal recognition of the women's role in the community and governance of the nation. Projects financed and resourced through the NRA could be tied into the educational and training programs discussed below. Here are some of the projects the Ngarrindjeri *miminar* discussed.

*A **Women's Place:*** We need a Meeting Place for Women where we can share stories, hold meetings and workshops, network, teach arts and crafts, create employment through activities like feather flowers, wood carving, weaving, swan egging, painting, jewellery making, store our weaving, and other cultural items, discuss needs such as child care, health care, Elder care, women's safety. In such a place women would gather to deliberate on issues. Their representatives on various committees could report and seek input, young girls could learn, and important cultural objects could be kept

Making feather flowers: Daisy Rankine, Edie Carter, Latoya Love and Emily Webster, Women's Review Weekend, January 14, 2006, Camp Coorong

Photograph: Vesper Tjukonai

safe. As with the idea of the *Tendi*, there are examples of women's places in the ethnographic literature (Bell 1998:272–5; Hemming 1997).

The young women were particularly enthusiastic about the development of 'cultural careers' and opportunities to develop strong trading relationships with international Indigenous women's groups. Current connections with women's artisans groups in Egypt and the Americas through Tourism Norway and The International Ecotourism Society (TIES) could be ways for Ngarrindjeri

women to develop an international profile as world-class Indigenous artisans. Aunty Ellen's weaving has been widely exhibited and there is a strong national and international interest in Ngarrindjeri weaving. The success of weaving classes at Camp Coorong is encouraging and weaving is a popular component of the eco-tourist activities offered to visitors. A Women's Place could be a springboard for 'cultural careers' in weaving and other crafts.

At a Women's Place, health issues

Beading: Eunice Aston and her sister Margaret Sumner and Eunice's daughter Jessie Aston, January 14, 2006, Camp Coorong

Photograph: Vesper Tjukonai

including reproductive health, substance abuse and rehabilitation, and trouble with the law could be discussed and plans developed that were sensitive to Ngarrindjeri cultural values and priorities.

We want to learn about women's health and our bodies in a way that teaches respect and builds self-esteem.

We'd like to have workshops that focus on holistic health practices including alternative therapies and medicine to deal with post-traumatic stress disorder.

We need a safe place where we can talk of the signs of abuse, get contraceptive advice, relationship training, legal and career advice.

At a Women's Place, young women could be mentored by their Elders; hear stories of how their parents and grandparents used their wits to survive; learn more of the ways in which women's knowledge and skills are a valued part of Ngarrindjeri society and more about their place as one of worth within the Ngarrindjeri Nation. The Women's Place would be where women's *miwi* was strong, a place underwritten by the stories of the past and a place that anticipates a strong future for Ngarrindjeri *miminar* within the Nation. It would be a place where women could stand strong together.

An Elders' Village: There was lively discussion about the need for Elder Care and where a centre or village might be located.

Where will we go when we are too old to look after ourselves?

It makes sense to have a centre or village in Murray Bridge – that's where the property and services are available, but people living at Victor Harbor would not want to be too far from their families and local networks.

Would people at Raukkan consider using a Murray Bridge Centre?

What about people living in the Goolwa area?

There may be a need for a number of smaller satellite centres so that people can stay close to family and resources with which they are familiar.

A Research Centre: As the NRA grows in strength and is able to commission research and to respond to the demands of various bodies and government departments for research, there will need to be a designated space to house research materials, researchers, reports and publications. There is already a considerable body of Ngarrindjeri related publications in circulation. If these were housed in a Research Centre, it could offer one access point for Indigenous and non-Indigenous researchers. Ngarrindjeri negotiations with the South Australian Museum regarding the basis upon which Ngarrindjeri cultural knowledge and materials would be managed by the Museum for and on behalf of the Ngarrindjeri stalled in 2004–5. A Research Centre could seek

Kungun Ngarrindjeri Yunnan agreements with the Museum and other research institutions. A Centre would also provide a forum where the innovative provisions for protecting intellectual property rights, as set out in the NRA constitution (see clause 6.2.12 above), could be fleshed out.

Weaving: Rita Lindsay Sr, June 24, 2007, Camp Coorong

Photograph: Diane Bell

Although both women and men will require such a facility, the women spoke of a space dedicated to women's needs. Partnerships with educational institutions like Flinders University, University of Adelaide and University of South Australia as well as with research institutes such as the CSIRO are already in progress. The particular needs of women need to be considered as these partnerships develop. New partnering possibilities could be explored for projects that are of direct concern to women and Ngarrindjeri Nation projects where women's needs and ideas should be taken into consideration.

Starter cabins: Along with a number of other women, Aunty Hilda Day was concerned about the needs of young couples who are just starting out: Staying at home breaks their spirit and they remain dependent, she said. One idea was for the NRA to build small cabins like those at Camp Coorong for young couples. These 'starter cabins' would be owned and managed by the NRA, might be situated out of town, and would provide independence from the extended family and an affordable start for young ones. One suggestion was that by being out of town, the young ones would be at a distance from the pub and other distractions and perhaps located in a village type development where Elders might also have accommodation. Others thought they would want to be in town. They should be given a choice, said Aunty Eileen McHughes.

Making feather flowers: Alice Abdulla and Jacinta Reid, Camp Coorong, May 2005

Photograph: Anne McMahon

A Ngarrindjeri Education and Training Centre: All present at the workshop placed a priority on the need for education and training and agreed that economic development plans needed to be built on education and training that was consistent with and supportive of Ngarrindjeri cultural values. Here are some of the Ngarrindjeri *miminar's* words.

A Ngarrindjeri Education and Training Centre would be a place where all could learn more of their history, their families, *laklinyerar*, and Nation.

Without skills we won't get decent jobs and we want real jobs. We need to be independent.

Young girls needed to stay at school so that they can get decent jobs and be able to look after themselves.

Elders need to provide role models for young people and to mentor them.

Young people, boys and girls, would learn respect for their Elders.

Education and training should be welcoming and supportive rather than intimidating and patronising.

Education and training should take account of the needs of mothers and grandmothers in terms of location, access and scheduling.

The women's vision was for a broad-based educational agenda spanning the generations: young people need encouragement to stay in school, adults need access to continuing education, especially literacy and numeracy, but also special job skills. All education and training needs to be within a framework that recognises the values and goals of the Ngarrindjeri Nation. It is hard to flourish when there is racism at school and in the workplace, so the women saw the need for cultural awareness training for teachers and employers to be part of any education and training program. It's not just telling people about our culture, it's changing their attitudes, Georgie Trevorrow said. And some of our own Indigenous workers could also benefit from learning more of their culture.

If there was a Ngarrindjeri Education and Training Centre sponsored by the NRA in partnership with employers and government departments, it would be possible to build educational programs that addressed the formal needs of children and adults while taking Ngarrindjeri cultural values into account. In terms of specialised courses, language could be taught alongside literacy and numeracy. There could be courses to develop women's management skills, courses on women's rights at law, women's health and others as the need arises. For school age children, the Centre could provide the out-of-school support needed to keep children in school by addressing Ngarrindjeri cultural identity and values. Young people need to know how to survive outside of school as well as in the classroom and playground, said Aunty Alice Abdulla.

Aunty Thelma Smart, Aunty Helen Jackson and Donna Kartinyeri said: Let's celebrate the young people who succeed. Let them know we are proud of them and that they are part of a proud nation of people. They need goals and they need discipline. They need to respect themselves, added Aunty Eileen McHughes. A number of the women mentioned the need to build self-esteem and Hilda Day said, Help them beat the shame. Shame is the spirit of fear. It only takes two or three words and they're down and it's hard to pick up again. Rita Jr added, They need a support base to keep them in school. The encouragement needs to come from within the school as well as from the families.

We need ways of linking the community programs into the schools. And with parents. They can only take so much before they lose the plot, Aunty Eileen adds. Too much fragmentation and working in different value frameworks. Our kids get targeted whenever there are problems at high school. There's only one who speaks up for them and mediates and we need a lot more of those kind of positions. And, says Audrey Lindsay, we need one in kindy, primary school, junior high school, middle high school. It's too much to ask of one AEW [Aboriginal Education Worker].

There are already a number of young Ngarrindjeri women and men at university and here there is further discussion about the possibilities of developing 'cultural careers'. One of the growing needs in Ngarrindjeri *ruwi* is for natural resource management officers who understand both the Ngarrindjeri law of the land and the bureaucratic demands of government departments. This is a career path the NRA could sponsor with scholarships, mentoring and by entering into partnerships with government and private enterprise.

A Ngarrindjeri Education and Training Centre could be part of the Research Centre already being contemplated by the NRA and it could coordinate programs with the Women's Place.

Places for children: Aunty Vicki Hartman: The most important time in learning is from zero to eight. They need that good start. When I see parents walking past, I say, "Are they going to kindy?" And I invite them to come in and see what we're doing, have a play. We have a big focus on language and Ngarrindjeri values. Then soon as they go to school, say in year one, they lose a lot of what they have learned. They lose their self-confidence and get lost. They put up their hand and no-one calls on them and then they start giving up. We teach them to be leaders in kindy and then they get to school and it's all different. Both my granddaughter and niece were really confident children and then they got to school and they hated it. Maybe we should have them till they're eight years old. And I'd go to school and tell the teachers if some of the kids had hearing problems or eye sight or things like that. That kind of liaison is really important. One of my nieces wanted to be a lawyer, but the teacher told her she wasn't brainy enough, said Aunty Eileen. Some of those kids are holy terrors before they go and then I see them after they've been to kindy and they're turned around.

And then there is the matter of child care. The *Minya Porlar* Creche attached to the Lower Murray Nungas Club offers places but more are needed. A number of young Ngarrindjeri women have ideas.

We need more space for child care. There's not enough spaces and that's a funding problem.

We want culturally appropriate child care where Ngarrindjeri kinship structures and values are taken into account. Kindergarten services are mainstreamed except at Raukkan and the crèche at Murray Bridge.

Kindy is good to get them ready for school. It's a gradual thing.

There are difficulties with the cost of attending and transport.

Aunty Eileen McHughes would like to see a program where young people could participate in activities that would teach them about their country and *ngatji* and teach them respect for themselves, their Elders, their stories, their country. It would be under Ngarrindjeri control and guided by Ngarrindjeri values. We might even think about 'student exchanges' with other Indigenous Nations, here and overseas.

Hopes for the future

There is no shortage of ideas. Central to plans for the future is a space, a Women's Place, where women can develop their plans in ways that suit their needs as women who care for their country, families and Ngarrindjeri Nation.

Edie Carter said: We've been given all this knowledge and we have to give something back. There's an expectation, the Old Fellars choose the young ones they want to carry the knowledge, but where are the young ones heading?

In their email stories, young Ngarrindjeri *miminar* spoke of the hopes for the future. Sisters Donna and Dorothy Kartinyeri (2007) wrote: We see the Ngarrindjeri nation standing high and being proud of who they are, being respected by everyone and inspiring others across the world to speak up for their culture and their beliefs; the Elders to take the time to pass on the knowledge and history of their culture e.g. language, story-telling, family tree and blood lines, living skills and their traditions. For the sake of past, present and future generations we want our history to be known.

I, Dorothy, would like to be a successful writer in poetry, an artist or a photographer. I, Donna, would like to be a successful poet, social worker or counsellor.

Georgie Trevorrow (2007) wrote: I see that we are a strong nation and we can put our differences aside and work as one to better our strength to fight for what we believe in. I see us getting what we want even if it takes a bit of time we will not let the government rule us and the telling us what to do will END. We are people with feelings and what the government doesn't know is that we are a strong nation and we will keep fighting til we get what we want no matter what obstacles they put up against us.

Kaysha Taylor: In the next five years I hope to walk out of the University of Adelaide with my Arts and Law degree. My interests stretch to Latin America where I hope to have the knowledge to travel and work with those who are less fortunate. And I am also very passionate about the Spanish language and community. But before I think about travelling to work over there I would love to stay within my community to help bring enthusiasm to faces that hardly ever smile. Every day I see my cousins and other family members who live their lives leading down hill. And every day I try to lead them on a path where they can be proud of themselves. I only hope that my accomplishment will somehow show my community what opportunities are out there.

In 2007, Rita Lindsay Jr was invited by the South Australian Education Department to explain to principals from across South Australia why Aboriginal Studies should be offered in schools and why the subject should remain within the school curriculum. In a speech delivered to the principals at the Dare to Lead Conference on Monday 19 March, 2007, she began by paying her respects to the Kaurna People, the traditional owners of the place where they were meeting. Rita Lindsay Jr (2007) continued:

As a young Ngarrindjeri Aboriginal woman I must say: "Why shouldn't schools offer Aboriginal Studies?"

I believe Aboriginal Studies has to be one of the most important parts of Australian, and therefore South Australian Education when teaching about Australian History, because Australian History did not start in 1788, and certainly South Australian history did not begin on South Australian Proclamation Day 1836.

If people don't want to learn about Aboriginal History, Heritage, Culture and Values then they are denying to themselves the single real opportunity of becoming a truly knowing and genuine Australian.

I have to challenge anyone here today, and anyone else in Australia, to give to us

Indigenous People a fair and just reason why schools should not offer Aboriginal Studies, because there is so much to learn...

One must find an honest and a truthful balance between each of our Indigenous and non-Indigenous educational requirements within the Australian education system that does not deny to the original people our rights to have our history acknowledged, maintained and taught within the Australian education system.

As a former Open Access Aboriginal Studies student, I gratefully appreciated the opportunity to enhance my knowledge and awareness of the issues facing Indigenous Australians in contemporary society. It also raised my self-esteem, confidence and identity by ceasing inverted racism. Studying this subject and working in collaboration with both non-Indigenous teachers and students inspired admiration and tolerance.

Finally, and most importantly to Reconciliation and to the survival of we the Indigenous people, for Australian Education to refuse to allow Aboriginal Studies to be taught in the education system is to continue to deny Aboriginal People their rightful place in the History of this Country, our birthright and homeland, and will allow for the unchanged continuation of ignorance and racism arising in part in the ongoing denial of the truth, justice, freedom and equity of our Ancient History and Connections to this Country.

Therefore, I ask you to take with you the thought that the continuity of Aboriginal Studies is essential for the sustainability of positive race relations for both present and future generations to come.

Thank you.

Ngarrindjeri *miminar* are not afraid of hard work. Ngarrindjeri *miminar* have ideas and know that they need to act. They have spoken openly and frankly of their lives, struggles, hopes and needs. There is an urgency to their words.

Asserting our
Ngarrindjeri Identity

If we get it right, our children will say, "This is what they wanted for us."
Aunty Ellen Trevorrow, 2007

In the June 22–24, 2007 workshop, we began our list of 'What do we want?' By the end of the second workshop we had several hundred items. Consolidating these items and sorting them into categories was done as a group activity by the women at the August 10–11, 2007 workshop and further refined on August 19, 2007. The order is for convenience sake and does not represent a hierarchy of needs or wants.

- Caring for Country: Culture, *miwi*, spirituality, passing on knowledge, language, history, telling the stories, art, crafts, dance, songs, cooking, learning kinship and *ngatji*, bush tucker and medicinal plants, stronger relationships and communities, respecting the law of the land.

- Self Governance: Acknowledgement of traditional/rightful owners of this land, respecting the law, education and training, employment, a women's board, youth advisory, well-being centre, research centre, family support, transport, valuing men, women and children, building a strong nation, financial management.

- Ngarrindjeri Nation – Independence: The Nation to own more land, more funding for Aboriginal communities: Place for Women, Birthing Centre, Units for Young, Elders' Village. More meeting places for confidential advice, appropriate housing, transport.

Back row: Vicki Hartman, Rita Lindsay Jr, Phyllis Williams, Helen Jackson, Thelma Smart, Audrey Lindsay

Middle row: Dylan Gibbs Trevorrow, Georgie Trevorrow, Diane Bell, Noreen Kartinyeri, Eileen McHughes holding Georgia Trevorrow, Jacob Trevorrow, Hank Trevorrow

Front row: Dorothy Kartinyeri holding Brendon Jackson, Donna Kartinyeri holding Phoebe Kartinyeri, Innes Jackson holding Peter Jackson.

Workshop Number Four, Camp Coorong, August 19, 2007

Photograph: Diane Bell

Glossary

Some Ngarrindjeri Terms[30]

Kaldowinyeri: The Creation

kringkari/kringkarar or *kringkri/kringkrar*: non-Indigenous person/people

Kumarangk: place of pregnancy, Hindmarsh Island

kungun: listen

laklinyeri/lakliyerar: clan/clans

meemini, mimini/miminar, (mi:mini/mi:mininar): woman/women

mingka: bird, messenger of death

miwi, mewi, (mi:wi): sixth sense, centre of being, feelings, emotions and knowledge, located in stomach, soul substance

mulyawongk: 'bunyip', creature who lives in caves and deep holes in the River Murray

Munjinggi Muntjinggi, Munjinggi, Mungingee, Muntjinggar, Mantjingga: Seven Sisters, Pleiades

ngatji/ngartji (nga:tji): totem, friend, county-man, protector

ngori: pelican

nukan (nakan): look

pondi: Murray Cod

porli/porlar (po:rli/po:rlar): child/children

prupi/prupe: evil spirit

Raukkan: Point McLeay, the old place *Rawulkan*

ringbalin: traditional dance

Ritjaruki: Willy wagtail

Rupelli (Ru:puli): Elected leader of the Ngarrindjeri Nation

ruwar: body

ruwi/ruwe (ru:wi): country, Ngarrindjeri land

Tendi: governing council of Ngarrindjeri Law

thunggallun yunti (thanggalun yunti): standing together

una? (ana?): isn't it?

yartooka (yatukar): young girls

yunnan (yanun): talking, speaking

Kungun and Yunnan:

Editor's Epilogue

Camp Coorong calling: What are you doing this weekend?
Are you busy?

Diane: Why? What's happening?

Diane's story

What was happening was a workshop in June 2007, the first of two, and Ellen Trevorrow was inviting me to be the facilitator. The workshops multiplied. This book grew from there.

Working with the Ngarrindjeri is always a joy. They live to tell stories: stories of their country, families and their Old People who have passed away; stories of their hopes for the future. Working with the Ngarrindjeri is also a constant reminder of the impact of two centuries of a non-Indigenous presence on those stories: the pain, anguish and loss; the survival in the face of abuse, ignorance and violence.

My first work with Ngarrindjeri was in the context of the struggle to protect *Kumarangk*, initially as a consultant on their application brought under the *Australian and Torres Strait Islander Heritage Protection Act, 1984*, and then as a researcher on *Ngarrindjeri Wurruwarrin: A world that is, was and will be* (Bell 1998). When the book was launched, Ngarrindjeri and their supporters took to the streets of Adelaide. As they marched to Parliament House to present a copy of the book to the Minister for Aboriginal Affairs, they chanted, We're not liars, and held the book aloft.

For the next several years I stayed in contact with my Ngarrindjeri friends, visited, emailed and appeared as an expert witness in the trial where the Ngarrindjeri were finally vindicated (von Doussa 2001). They were no liars. During that period I was living in the USA, but now I am home, home in Ngarrindjeri *ruwi* [country]. Living in direct contact with the traditional owners holds out the opportunity to negotiate how one may be at home in someone else's country. Here I know the names of the birds. I watch *ngori* [pelican] fishing in the river on which I live. I pay attention to the rapid movements of the *ritjaruki* [Willy wagtail] raising their second brood for the year just outside my kitchen window. What message does it carry? Then one day it stands stock still on my back verandah. I follow its gaze and see a brown snake slithering along the groove between the paving stones, just where I was about to step.

Living in Ngarrindjeri country is a choice I made when I decided to leave the USA after seventeen years as professor at several different universities and liberal arts colleges. I had said I would leave if President George Bush was re-elected in 2004. He was. I left. I also made a decision to keep working with Ngarrindjeri and, because this part of the country is experiencing a severe drought, I have participated in local community actions addressing the future health of the River, Lakes and Coorong. Ngarrindjeri *ngatji* have been telling us for a long time that the River is in a bad way. As the Ngarrindjeri *miminar* say in this book: We need more *kungun* and more *yunnan*. We need to stand together.

Women's workshops 2007

How were the workshops organised? What did we do? How did the stories get onto the pages? Working on this book has been an opportunity to build on and refine the methodology of the dialogical research method developed in my earlier work with the Ngarrindjeri (see Bell 1998:366–371). In that project, I sat with each person whose story appeared in the book, checked details and added more stories. Those who had worked with me on that project knew there would be many opportunities to reread and discuss their stories before the book was finalised. It had been a respectful dialogue and each had learned more of the other. Generally the feedback came from family groups but I did not have the opportunity to workshop the whole text with larger groups that crossed generational and family lines. And I did not have the opportunity to work with many younger women. The workshops of 2007 made it possible to experiment with different ways of writing with the Ngarrindjeri women and we had access to a range of technologies that facilitated and enriched the feedback aspect of the research.

Workshop one: On the weekend of June 22–24, 2007, thirty women responded to the invitation from the NLPA to participate in a workshop at Camp Coorong. On the Friday evening, we were welcomed by Uncle Tom and Aunty Ellen Trevorrow and briefed by Steve Hemming who had been working with the male leadership team on the new governance structure. The night was chilly. The wind was raging. After the *yunnan*, I snuggled into my sleeping bag with my hot water bottle and made notes for the next day. I shouldn't have worried: Ellen beat me to it. She had four questions ready. We ate breakfast, more women arrived. The fire warmed the room. Our work began.

We wrote the questions suggested by Aunty Ellen on the big white board, talked together as a group and then broke into small discussion groups at the tables. Each table had a note taker and a person to report on the deliberations. As a general rule, the women sat in family-based groups. Children sat quietly on the lap of a mother, aunt, grandmother, or to one side on the couch.

The younger women, or the person with the neatest handwriting, took notes. Initially it was the older women who provided the summary overviews at the end of each session but that began to change as we moved to the social issues with which younger women were grappling. We had two sessions in the morning and two in the afternoon and a general debriefing in the evening. We talked about caring for country, governance and the NRA, economic development, treaty-making, repatriation and a host of social issues. The Federal Government take-over of Northern Territory communities had just been announced and the response was visceral: Hands off our children.

That first workshop set the tone for following ones. They were intense and the matters weighty. We also took lots of breaks and drank many cups of tea. The smokers had their own space in the weak winter sun outside the building and on a number of occasions we non-smokers joined them, just to make sure we didn't miss any of the ideas being discussed. I was not able to stay for the Sunday session of the first workshop, so Annie Vanderwyk and Ellen Trevorrow ran those. I worked from the notes the women had written on the big sheets of paper and checked back for direct quotations as needed.

During the next week, Annie Vanderwyk and I typed up the women's words from the notes on the large sheets of paper. We exchanged emails and asked follow up questions. I talked more with Aunty Ellen Trevorrow and brothers Uncle Tom and Uncle George Trevorrow about what they, in their role as chairs of key Ngarrindjeri committees, hoped for from the project. Those issues were added to the list for the second workshop. At that stage we had a report. It needed some background, so I went back to the sources on Ngarrindjeri history and culture, found material that complemented the stories the women had told at the workshops, located some old photographs and downloaded the ones from the weekend. Via email, Annie and I hammered out a draft of what we had so far.

Workshop two: At the July 5–6, 2007, workshop, the draft in hardcopy was read by Aunty Ellen Trevorrow, Aunty Alice Abdulla, Aunty Rita Lindsay, Edie Carter, Annie Vanderwyk, Aunty Adeline Smith, Aunty Eileen McHughes, Aunty Vicki Hartman, Aunty Millie Rigney, Kaysha Taylor and Anne McMahon. We read it aloud: each woman read her own story. More stories were forthcoming. The women wrote their corrections, amendments and further comments directly onto the draft. At that point it was clear there would be a lively discussion about how to spell Ngarrindjeri words (see p. 109). It was also clear as women read their individual stories that we would be using Ngarrindjeri respect terms throughout (see p. 110). Reading aloud was an opportunity to see if the spoken words, as transcribed, worked as written words. For the most part, the story-tellers liked the sense that the texts captured the flavour and liveliness of the spoken words, but on others, they wanted to edit for sense, accuracy and to add further details. Being able to craft their speech so that it reads 'properly' is welcomed. Ngarrindjeri are all too familiar with being misreported or made to look foolish, or, as in the case of *Kumarangk*, portrayed as liars. My experience of Ngarrindjeri story-telling is that people are scrupulous about not appropriating the words of another, are careful to say with whom the story originated, and engage listeners by saying, *Una* [isn't it?] and then proceeding.

Aunty Ellen Trevorrow had been working on a title for the project and a cover design concept that incorporated the Seven Sisters. Her design concept was approved by the meeting. Aunty Eileen McHughes made sure we used *miminar* [women], the Ngarrindjeri plural of *mimini* [woman] and not *miminis*, as in the English rendering of the plural. Uncle Tom Trevorrow had suggestions regarding historic documents that might be included such as the 1923 'Save our Children' petition and these were also approved. There was more time for story-telling, small group discussion and reporting. The notes from the tables were more detailed than at the earlier workshop and I used a small digital recorder as back up. The conversations were dense and intense. The young women were in full voice. They asked for stories from their Elders about what it was like for them growing up in the fringe camps. Their Elders talked about the new threats, their anguish over lives lost to drugs and alcohol.

The expanded draft incorporating materials from the second workshop had grown beyond a report. Could it be a book? Spinifex Press was prepared to work with the Ngarrindjeri Lands and Progress Association to produce a larger print run of *Kungun Ngarrindjeri Miminar Yunnan* than would have been possible had it remained a report. However, as a book, more editing, some restructuring and further research was required. So Aunty Ellen Trevorrow helped convene another workshop.

Workshop three: On August 10–11, 2007, we gathered once more to read and discuss the next draft that I'd prepared. We began the day by discussing the August 1, 2007, judgement of Justice Thomas Gray in the case of Bruce Trevorrow, the first member of the Stolen Generations to be awarded compensation. Would it be appealed?[31] What were the implications for others who were stolen, institutionalised, adopted and fostered?

After morning tea, at the invitation of the women, the Ngarrindjeri male leaders, who had also been meeting at Camp Coorong, joined us. They

Workshop Three: Meeting with the men, Camp Coorong, August 10, 2007

Back row: Vicki Hartman, Grant Rigney, Julie Carter, Edie Carter, Steve Hemming, Darryle Rigney, Luke Trevorrow, Christopher Wilson

Middle row: Eileen McHughes, Adeline Smith, Ellen Trevorrow, Noreen Kartinyeri, Rita Lindsay, Matthew Rigney

Front row: Donna and Dorothy Kartinyeri

Photograph: Diane Bell

provided an update on the new governance structure and Uncle Matt Rigney asked that the women have input to the NRA. The conversation continued over lunch. The women were pleased that the exchange had been possible and that they had already considered the NRA and were ready to offer their views.

The Ngarrindjeri readily use technology to facilitate their decision-making. They are familiar with Powerpoint presentations and particularly adept at working together on texts on the computer. So after lunch, page by page, we worked through the text projected onto a big screen. The meeting was set down for two days but Uncle Tom Trevorrow had been taken to hospital on August 9, and his sisters Aunty Alice and Aunty Rita and wife Aunty Ellen wanted to return to Adelaide to be with him. So the women agreed to call it a day and reconvene for one last time on August 19, 2007.

Workshop four: On August 19, 2007, we had a near to final draft to workshop. Once again we read together from the screen and the women made corrections and of course, told more stories. One highlight of that workshop was the writing of the Prologue by the women present. After many weeks of working together, there was a general ease with each other and we were well aware of what each could contribute. The women spoke the words. I typed them into the computer. The women read them from the screen. They searched for the right words to express their ideas, the most apt turn of phrase, made sure everyone had input, and enjoyed some light-hearted moments with close kin. The text quickly took shape. The sentences flowed. We read the text out loud together, set it down for a cuppa and returned to polish the words.

We decided we'd try to reduce the list of hundreds of items that were on the 'What do we want?' list that we'd started during the first workshops and pulled together at the third workshops. Each woman had a printed copy of the list. Over dinner family groups at each table began the task of getting rid of duplicates, grouping like items together and checking we had not missed anything. After dinner, we edited the list on the screen, tried various headings, and eventually settled on 'Caring for Country', 'Self-governance', and 'Ngarrindjeri Nation'. Everything fell into place.

During the fourth workshop, the older women encouraged the younger women to tell more of their stories. I followed up on the day but the younger women had pressing responsibilities with children and couldn't stay. "Do you have email?" I asked. Over the next couple of weeks, sisters Donna and

Dorothy Kartinyeri (2007), Rita Lindsay Jr (2007), Georgie Trevorrow (2007) and Kaysha Taylor (2007) emailed me their stories. Conversations about the book moved online. We needed another workshop to talk about how these stories would be incorporated.

Ngarrindjeri Miminar Gathering, October 2–4, 2007: Fortunately, the Lower Murray Nungas Club had organised a three-day gathering at Camp Coorong and Eunice Aston was happy to incorporate a session on the book as part of the planned activities. The gathering commenced with *Ngarrindjeri Miminar Ringbalin*, a Ngarrindjeri women's ceremony to cleanse and heal, that was led by Rita Lindsay Jr. Her songs called us together, the ground reverberated as she danced, the smoke trailed through Camp Coorong cleansing the venue and each participant. Over the following days, there were sessions on women's health and alternative therapies, activity tables for feather flowers, weaving and beading, bush-food walks, videos and an evening concert for Ngarrindjeri musicians, poets and story-tellers. I listened,

Ngarrindjeri *Miminar* Gathering, Camp Coorong, October 2–4, 2007

Back row: Nola Richardson, Leilani Mallie, Alice Abdulla, Ellen Trevorrow, Diane Bell, Cassie Rigney, Eunice Aston, Rita Lindsay Jr, Noreen Kartinyeri, Sharon Forrester, Thelma Smart, Dorothy Shaw, Avril Faint

Middle row: Rita Lindsay, Gloria Sparrow, Diane Groves, Audrey Lindsay

Front row: Joy-Anne Wilson holding Savannah Walker, Tori-Lee, Innes (Ninny) Rigney, Kathleen Faint (in front of Audrey), Krystal Weetra with Destiny Shaw and Chase Rigney.

Photograph: Vesper Tjukonai

took notes, read them back to the speakers and another form of story entered the book.

This gathering was another opportunity to discuss the book. Once again more stories were forthcoming. More details needed checking. New questions arose. Should we include the foundational stories of the Ngarrindjeri Nation? The story of *Ngurunderi's* creation of the River Murray marks out Ngarrindjeri *ruwi* and Law. The story of the *Muntjinggar* [Seven Sisters or Pleiades], traces the passage from girlhood to womanhood in Ngarrindjeri *ruwi*. Over the next few weeks, I went back to the sources again, talked more with the Ngarrindjeri leadership and, because this section concerned the histories of the whole Ngarrindjeri Nation, sought input from the men who had worked on the *Yarluwar-Ruwe Plan* (Ngarrindjeri Tendi *et al* 2006).

After the workshops: Once we had concluded the group sessions, I worked on various sections of the book with specific individuals. We talked on the telephone. I visited wherever possible. I took every opportunity at meetings on other matters, to check facts with knowledgeable people. More stories. I had been interested in the painting of the spider by Audrey Lindsay that hangs in the Museum at Camp Coorong. Once again technology came to the fore. Through her daughter, Rita Jr, who works at Camp Coorong, I arranged to talk to Audrey about the painting. Over the telephone, Audrey explained the meaning of the symbols. I typed it up, read it back to her, emailed it to her daughter, and there was the women's story that showed how the foundational stories of *Ngurunderi*, the Seven Sisters and *Wururi* were connected.

The Ngarrindjeri have a rich photographic archive to which those who work with the Ngarrindjeri have contributed and on which I was able to draw. More than once I asked a question along the lines of "Who is that child with her back to the camera?" The identification process involved recalling the day the photograph was taken, finding other photographs taken on the day and tracking through whose children and grannies were present. Once the family lines were established, there was discussion across the generations to make sure the names were correct and then telephone calls and emails to make sure we had the spelling right.

During the workshops, I had cleared the photographs I had taken but I also wanted to consult about the captions. When I asked Rita Lindsay Jr about the photographs of her performance of October 2, 2007, she talked about the materials she had used and the meaning of the *ringbalin* [traditional dance]. She thought about how much should properly be revealed and then emailed me her exegesis of the performance (Lindsay 2008). It is reproduced in Chapter Two.

I wanted to talk more with Aunty Eileen about the Ngarrindjeri language. We sat at her dining table as children came home from school, talked about their day, ate a healthy snack and sat down to do their homework. Aunty Eileen brought out a folder of important documents, each in a protective plastic sleeve so we could get the title of her language courses correct. A week later she phoned me with further details about a source we'd been discussing.

During visits to Camp Coorong in November and December, I was able to talk more with people visiting the Camp and the Ngarrindjeri who live and work there. Our conversations were wide ranging and more sources were forthcoming. Do you know about Blandowski's travels and drawings? Uncle Tom asked me and produced the document prepared by Harry Allen (2006). We pored over the drawings and pondered the Ngarrindjeri names Blandowski cites. A number of people came and went and each offered an insight.

It takes time for these conversations to occur and time is a scarce commodity when it comes to many of the 'consultations' that occur with Indigenous Australians. The all too familiar pattern is one where the consultant arrives with a list of questions and takes the answers away. The community is used as a resource to be mined for information. Feedback and negotiation is minimal. Another report is generated. Our workshops, conversations and negotiations were held over a period of seven months and a number of Ngarrindjeri, young, old, female and male, worked on this book.

The sources

In *Kungun Ngarrindjeri Miminar Yunnan*, Ngarrindjeri women's stories frame the text. They come to us from a variety of sources. Most vivid are the stories of the current generation of knowledgeable women. Aunty Alice Abdulla and her older sister Aunty Rita Lindsay bring the wisdom and the struggle of a generation who grew up in the fringe camps to their stories. Audrey Lindsay paints the stories. Aunty Ellen Trevorrow is a Ngarrindjeri cultural weaver who has been running workshops at Camp Coorong for over a decade. Aunty Eileen McHughes is not afraid to speak her mind and her words carry real weight. Aunty Eunice Aston along with younger women such as Edie Carter, Rita Lindsay Jr, Donna and Dorothy Kartinyeri, Kaysha Taylor and Georgie

Trevorrow speak with respect of their Elders as they write about how they each balance the demands of home, work and study with their Ngarrindjeri heritage. Their world is deeply scarred by the incursion of drugs into local communities and towns.

The women's stories illuminate the distinctive roles and responsibilities they have as members of the Ngarrindjeri Nation. They emphasise their concern for their country, the future of their families, their health and well-being. The Elders want to see more opportunities for young women in terms of education and training. Younger women, who are pursuing higher education, travelling interstate and overseas, working in health care, education and on various cultural projects find inspiration in the wisdom of their Elders, many of whom did not complete high school. The analyses of these women, young and old, of the current socio-economic and political situation are astute, their suggestions for a way forward practical.

At each generation, the Ngarrindjeri have had their public intellectuals whose ideas have helped shape the understandings of the broader society of Indigenous matters. In this book we hear from respected Elders such as Aunty Maggie Jacobs (1920–2003), Aunty Veronica Brodie (1941–2007) and Dr Doreen Kartinyeri (1935–2007). Their stories come to us through their own publications (Brodie 2007; Kartinyeri 1983, 1985, 1989, 1990, 1996, 2006), from interviews with researchers, the media and government departments and through documents produced for legal proceedings. In choosing stories from the Old People to include in this book, we have looked to those authored by Ngarrindjeri themselves. Aunty Leila Rankine's (1932–1993) articles and poetry celebrate her love of country and provide a critique of the assimilation era (Rankine 1974, c1980). Then there are fragments like the text of Aunty Annie Rankine (1969) about everyday life and Ngarrindjeri beliefs and practices. Where appropriate we have included stories from men. David Unaipon (1872/3–1967), the first published Aboriginal author, was Ngarrindjeri and amongst his stories, written down in the 1920s, is one of the coming of age rituals for Ngarrindjeri women (Unaipon 1925). Through the field notes, tape recordings and publications of a range of visitors to Ngarrindjeri *ruwi*, we hear the voices of other Ngarrindjeri sages, such as Old Clarence Long (Milerum 1869–1941) in Norman Tindale's papers (Tindale and Long nd); Albert Karloan (1864–1940) and Margaret 'Pinkie' Mack (1858–1954) in the work of Catherine and Ronald Berndt (Berndt R. 1940; Berndt *et al* 1993; Berndt C. 1994a and b). More recently, Ngarrindjeri men and women speak to us through collaborative research projects (Bell 1998; Hemming 1985, 1994a, 1994b, Hemming *et al* 1989; Kartinyeri and Anderson 2008; Ngarrindjeri Tendi *et al* 2006).

As the Bibliography to this book indicates, there are many accounts of Ngarrindjeri history and culture and Ngarrindjeri read these texts critically. They are familiar with what has been written about them and have opinions on its accuracy and authenticity and are alive to ethical lapses by researchers. They shift through the sources, pay attention to when, where and from whom the information was gleaned and trace their relationships to the 'informant'. Ngarrindjeri recognise the power of the written word and are acutely aware that it can be used to dismiss and demean their culture. So, over the past five years or so, the Ngarrindjeri leadership has paid serious attention to the way in which research about Ngarrindjeri is conducted and presented. One strategy has been to present and to publish papers that are an interplay of Indigenous and non-Indigenous voices (Hemming *et al* 2007). This practice has given rise to grounded discussions of the ethics of research and new forms of story-telling and cultural critique. Another strategy has been to enter into *Kungun Ngarrindjeri Yunnan* (Listen to Ngarrindjeri People Talking) agreements. Through the newly incorporated Ngarrindjeri Regional Authority, the concept of intellectual property rights has been expanded so that it takes in Ngarrindjeri concepts of cultural property.

Spelling Ngarrindjeri words

Which spellings would be used in this book has been the subject of intense discussion with a number of speakers of the Ngarrindjeri language, especially those who grew up hearing the language spoken. After much discussion, we have retained the spellings used in the written materials of the Ngarrindjeri Lands and Progress Association (NLPA). Since its incorporation in 1985, the NLPA has been teaching the Ngarrindjeri language and their spelling system is one that makes intuitive sense to Ngarrindjeri who are literate in English. There are regional differences in pronunciation on which the older generation remark and different renderings of the same word may reflect these subtle differences. Words carry identities. There is, as Ngarrindjeri remark, a certain 'lilt' to the speech of specific families. Ngarrindjeri are concerned that the language be treated with respect and that it remain under Ngarrindjeri control. Its survival is a matter of pride. Ngarrindjeri language is part of Ngarrindjeri culture.

Ngarrindjeri concern for their language was noted by the Rev. George Taplin (1878:6) who wrote of those he called "Narrinyeri": "The aborigines speak their language very correctly." The language has proved to be a hard one to write down. The Ngarrindjeri became literate in English very early and their ways of spelling their words offer insights regarding some of the unique sounds of their language that do not occur in English. When asked to write a word, Ngarrindjeri usually repeat the word over and over, consult with each other, and then offer English equivalents. But the prime consideration, as in Taplin's time, remains the pronunciation.

Visitors to Ngarrindjeri country have used a variety of spelling systems, from the work of early missionaries such as Taplin (1859–79; 1873; 1878; 1879) and H.E.A.Meyer (1843), through anthropologists Ronald and Catherine Berndt (Berndt *et al* 1993) and Norman Tindale (1931–4, nd), to linguists like Colin Yallop and C. Grimwade (1975) and Maryalyce McDonald (2002). Today Ngarrindjeri is being taught in Murray Bridge at the local school using an orthography that offers a consistent way of rendering the language (Gale and French 2007).[32] However, without being familiar with the system that underlies the new orthography, there is no guarantee that someone who has not heard the words would be able to pronounce them simply from reading the new spelling.

In time, the familiar spellings may yield to the logic of the new. For now, it is important that Ngarrindjeri words are in use, that there is a younger generation keen to learn the language and an older generation who knows how to pronounce the words and has the will to work on language programs.

Respect terms and kinship: The Ngarrindjeri cultural way

Distinctive Ngarrindjeri ways of speaking to and about close family, more distant relatives and those who have passed away, embody central values of their culture and recall aspects of their contact histories. As Ngarrindjeri readily admit, their way can be confusing to others but it is disrespectful, rude and even dangerous to address a person by their first name alone. Elder Tom Trevorrow explains: Within Ngarrindjeri society the terms of Uncle, Aunty, Brother, Sister, Grandmother or Grandfather are used by individual persons when they see, feel and identify with a particular person upon whom they bestow the title. When the time is right to bestow a title, an inner feeling in your *miwi* tells you the time is right to bestow that title. You feel good about that person. You know. It just comes automatically. This is the Ngarrindjeri cultural way.

Throughout the book, we have followed the Ngarrindjeri cultural way.

There is the respect due to one's Elders. In everyday speech and in story-telling, honorifics such as 'Aunty' or 'Aunt', 'Uncle', 'Nanna', 'Granny' and 'Grandfather' are routinely used. For the status of 'Elder' to be bestowed, a person needs not only to be old enough (around fifty), but also to be wise and to be seen as part of the Ngarrindjeri community.

Ngarrindjeri who passed away some time ago are known collectively as the 'Old People'. Repatriation and reburial of the Old People currently in museums and other institutions within Australia and abroad is a priority for the Ngarrindjeri Nation. Great offence is given by speaking of the Old People as skeletal remains or bones.

When speaking of a particular deceased person, such as David Unaipon (1872/3–1967), Ngarrindjeri will say 'that Old Fellar', or use a term that reflects their relationship to the person. Similarly when referring to an important woman, such as Louisa Karpany (1821–1921), they will say 'that Old Girl', or call her 'Granny Louisa'.

There are also important 'Old People' who may be referred to as 'Queen' as with 'Queen Louisa' for Louisa Karpany and 'Queen Ethel' for Granny Ethel Wympie Watson. These titles are drawn from the colonial experience but the recognition of these women as cultural authorities is embedded in Ngarrindjeri social structure.

Ngarrindjeri also use the kinship terms 'Aunty', 'Uncle', sometimes shortened to 'Unc', 'Brother' ('Bro'), 'Sister' ('Sis'), 'Cousin' ('Cuz'), 'Nanna', or 'Pop' for persons who stand in that blood relationship to them. For brothers-in-law, the term *ronggi* is often used. The kin to whom these terms apply is wider than the nuclear family and the terminology takes seniority of lineages and marriage lines into account. The terms serve to locate every Ngarrindjeri person within a kin network and thereby individuals are able to assert a shared identity as Ngarrindjeri. The terms may be used to incorporate non-Ngarrindjeri people within the reach of Ngarrindjeri sociality.

Children are taught to use terms as matters of respect and as ways of locating themselves within Ngarrindjeri kinship networks as they are learning to speak.

Standing together

The workshops provided an interesting model for thinking about how women and men might be part of decision-making and governance of the Ngarrindjeri Nation. When the women were meeting, the men kept their distance. It was a matter of respect. No-one said, 'Keep out'. Rather, the women were being supported in their workshop activities by the men, but at a distance. The women were doing their part in working for the Ngarrindjeri Nation by taking the issues of caring for country, governance and economic development seriously. They were exercising their responsibility as citizens of the Ngarrindjeri Nation. During the tea breaks, over lunch and dinner, there were lively interactions between the men and women. Sisters and brothers, husbands and wives, cousins, uncles, nieces, nephews and aunts talked, checked details, proposed more questions. Between the workshops the discussions continued.

In terms of young and old, once again the workshops offered insights for a model for working across the generations. The younger women were confident in reading the notes taken at their table discussions. Their Elders supported them and praised their presentations. In one of the story-telling sessions, the young women were forthright in saying what they wanted to ask their Elders and their Elders were equally forthcoming in answering their questions and posing their own. The older women were comfortable in telling their stories in a face-to-face situation. They grew up in an oral culture where the spoken word carries weight, where one knows who has been told the story. The younger women, familiar with oral story-telling traditions but also at home with electronic communications, turned to email to tell their stories. Once again, the process took time.

The Ngarrindjeri Nation has forged links with First Peoples in North America, entered into partnerships with government departments and universities, undertaken joint research projects, and negotiated agreements with local councils and action groups. Women have been important in these ventures, as weavers, ambassadors, mentors, and researchers. Ngarrindjeri *miminar* have a long history of speaking out against injustice, especially with respect to the removal of their children. They have fought to protect their sacred places, been vilified and been vindicated. Despite the intense and at times hostile scrutiny of Ngarrindjeri culture (Brunton 1999; Hill 1999; Kenny 1996), despite the removal of children (Wilson 1997), grave robbing and desecration of sacred places (Berndt *et al* 1993:16; Wilson 2005), Ngarrindjeri women and men stand tall. The leadership is dedicated to ensuring a future for the Ngarrindjeri Nation.

In 2007, a number of projects came to fruition and once again women contributed. In March 2007, *Yarluwar-Ruwe Plan* (*Sea Country Plan*) was launched at Goolwa by Jay Weatherill, South Australian Minister for Families and Communities, Aboriginal Affairs and Reconciliation, Housing, Ageing, Disability. Henceforth, all those having business with the Ngarrindjeri had a place where they could find first-hand accounts of Ngarrindjeri history, culture, and plans for the care of their country. The *Plan* noted that both men and women "have always been involved, and continue to be involved, in passing down our knowledge between generations and in decision-making about Ngarrindjeri affairs, land, waters and resources" (Ngarrindjeri Tendi *et al* 2006:12). In April 2007, the NRA was incorporated. A place was designated within the NRA for representation of women's concerns. In addition to the *Yarluwar-Ruwe Plan* and the NRA, Ngarrindjeri leaders had also been working in conjunction with Flinders University, the CSIRO and Charles Sturt University on a collaborative research project that looks at the connection between water, water-related resources and Ngarrindjeri well-being (Birckhead *et al* 2007). Yet again women attended the CSIRO associated workshops along with their menfolk.

Negotiations about the cover design for this book, shone light on another sort of 'standing together': a partnership between a trade publisher and the Ngarrindjeri leadership and story-tellers. Spinifex Press was dedicated to the principle that Ngarrindjeri women should be the decision-makers. They were firm that intellectual property rights and moral rights remained with the Ngarrindjeri story-tellers and were prepared to enter into a *Kungun Ngarrindjeri Yunnan* agreement with the Ngarrindjeri. The NLPA was to hold copyright. Spinifex listened carefully to the Ngarrindjeri cover concept: superimpose an image of the Seven Sisters in the night sky on a background mat of the circular weaving pattern that has become a Ngarrindjeri signature for their publications and reports. This cover had to satisfy a number of parties. It had to be culturally appropriate, attractive and inviting. We went back and forth: designer, editor, publisher, and Ngarrindjeri *miminar* and leadership. Each party had their own decision-making process. "We showed the range of designs to a number of people and this was the one everyone liked best," to I'm only one person. I need to talk to my Elders. The Elders looked to their stories, set out their priorities as Ngarrindjeri *miminar* and then sought input from the NLPA. The men took counsel from the Ngarrindjeri Rupelli. We had a cover. The final negotiations occurred during the record breaking Adelaide heat wave of March 2008. We were all worn down but we continued to talk, to try different designs and to respect the needs of each party. It took time but it was worth it. Future negotiations will build on the experience.

In *Kungun Ngarrindjeri Miminar Yunnan,* Ngarrindjeri women are standing together with each other and their menfolk in caring for their lands, waters, culture, families, and future. Their words complement and expand the ideas contained in the *Yarluwar-Ruwe Plan.* Their hopes for the future indicate the potential of the newly incorporated Ngarrindjeri Regional Authority. The attention to the concept of 'well-being' draws on the CSIRO project. The chairpersons of Ngarrindjeri committees, all men, who have taken the initiative in the *Yarluwar-Ruwe Plan*, the NRA and the CSIRO project (Rupelli, Uncle George Trevorrow of the Ngarrindjeri Tendi and the Ngarrindjeri Governance Working Group; Uncle Tom Trevorrow of the Ngarrindjeri Heritage Committee and the Ngarrindjeri Land and Progress Association; Uncle Matt Rigney of the Ngarrindjeri Native Title Management Committee) have met with the women as part of this project and see the women's workshops as an integral part of building a strong Ngarrindjeri Nation.

The workshops could have continued into 2008 and already plans are being hatched for further publications. This book is a beginning. Ngarrindjeri women need further time to deliberate, strategise and implement their ideas. The discussions thus far have been thoughtful and productive. There is an ongoing need for further Ngarrindjeri *Miminar* gatherings to be held at other places like Murray Bridge, Raukkan, Adelaide, Goolwa and Mannum.

Negotiations concerning the texts, oral and written, the cover, and the research strategies pursued for this book are part of what Ngarrindjeri women have to say and are part of developing ways of listening: *yunnan* and *kungun.* So much has been written *about* the Ngarrindjeri. This book has been an opportunity to write *with* the Ngarrindjeri and to make a further contribution to the Ngarrindjeri research, writing and publication agenda.

Thank you for your wit, insights, reflections, honesty, advice, questions, and trust.

Endnotes

1   Throughout the text the words of Ngarrindjeri, be they direct speech, published texts or emails, appear in a sans serif typeface. Quotations taken directly from the workshops appear as 2007 and quotations from email stories of participants are cited *pers. comm.* from the author to Diane Bell.

2   Under Section 11a of the *Aborigines Act*, 1934–1939, the Aborigines Protection Board (APB) could issue an exemption certificate if, in the opinion of the APB, an Aboriginal person "by reason of his character and standard of intelligence and development" was suitable and once exempted that person "shall cease to be an aborigine" for the duration of the declaration. See Mattingley and Hampton (1988: 48–52) and Department of Education (1990:171–2) for commentary from Aboriginal people who often referred to these certificates as "dog licences".

3   We had completed our workshops before the February 13, 2008 apology of the Australian Parliament to the Stolen Generations was delivered (see inside back cover). We hope our stories can be part of the journey of healing that lies ahead.

4   This book is to be read as complementary to *Yarluwar-Ruwe Plan* (Ngarrindjeri Tendi *et al* 2006). See Epilogue, p. 112-4 for more about the gendered dynamics of decision-making.

5   See Bell 1998:45. The poetics and politics of Ngarrindjeri story-telling have been explored at some length, particularly in the context of *Kumarangk* (Hindmarsh Island), but also with reference to exhibits and publications regarding Ngarrindjeri culture (see Bell 2001; Clarke 1995, 1997; Department of Education 1990; Hemming 1994b, 1996, 1997; Hemming *et al* 1989; Mattingley and Hampton 1988; Pearson 1998; Simons 2003). Also see the Epilogue for further discussion of the writing process.

6   The case pitted women who claimed they did not know the story of the sacred places against those who knew the story (Brodie 2007; Wilson 1998). The authenticity of the story was further contested in the media (Brunton 1999; Hill 1999; Kenny 1996; Simons 2003), by anthropologists (Bell 1998, 2001, 2007; Fergie 1994, 1996; Hemming 1996; von Doussa 2001), in the courts (Mead 1995; Stevens 1995; von Doussa 2001), parliament (Saunders 1994; Mathews 1996), and the museum (von Doussa 2001).

7   The 'Lies. Lies. Lies' headline of the Adelaide *Advertiser* of December 22, 1995, has wide currency. Reporting of the von Doussa decision was more muted.

8   See Fergie 1994, 1996; Saunders 1994 re the first Heritage application; Hemming 1996; Mead 1995; Stevens 1995 re the Royal Commission; Bell 1998; Simons 2003 re the second Heritage application.

9   *Wilson v Minister for Aboriginal and Torres Strait Islander Affairs* (1996) 189 CLR 1, challenged the ability of a Chapter III judge to report to the federal minister under the Heritage Act. It was not that the court thought Justice Mathews was not impartial but that there could be an appearance that the judge, appointed by the Minister, would be acting as his agent.

10 *Kartinyeri & Anor v. Commonwealth ('Hindmarsh Island Bridge* case') (1998) 195 CLR 337

11 The Chapmans sued the Commonwealth and others for compensation for delays in building the bridge. Their appeal against the decision of 2001 was dropped in 2002. Judge Von Doussa's findings stand uncontested. See *Thomas Lincoln Chapman and Ors v Luminis Pty Ltd, 088 127 085 and Ors*, Federal Court of Australia, No. SG 33 OF 1997.

12 Also spelled *ruwe; ngatji* also spelled *ngartji*. See Epilogue, p. 109-10 for note on spelling Ngarrindjeri words.

13 For discussion and further details of various aspects and tellings of *Ngurunderi* story see Bell (1998); Berndt R. (1940); Clarke (1994, 1995); Hemming (1994b); Hemming *et al* (1989); Meyer (1846); Penny (1842); Taplin (1873); Tindale (nd); Tindale and Long (nd); Unaipon (1990).

14 The Seven Sisters (Pleiades) is an open (or galactic) cluster that is associated with young women in a number of cultures. At the age of several hundred millions years, it is about a tenth of the age of the solar system and thus may be thought of as an adolescent of the skyworld. With magnification, thousands of stars can be seen but with the naked eye only six or seven are clearly visible. It is interesting that Ngarrindjeri make mention of six or seven and have an explanation for the seventh.

15 Many of these legends, with very minor variations, were published under the name of Ramsay Smith (1930, see also Bell 1998:129–131; Muecke and Shoemaker 2001). See Jones' (1989; 1993) critiques of Unaipon as representative of Ngarrindjeri culture and Simons' (2003:431–2) discussion of Unaipon (1924–5) as a Ngarrindjeri source. I address the issues raised by these critiques in a forthcoming article (see also Bell 1998:126–8, 497–8, 580; 2001).

16 I first showed Doreen Kartinyeri the Unaipon material in June 1997 along with materials from the Tindale collection in the South Australian Museum. When she read the World of Milerum (Tindale and Long nd), she noted how it resonated with what she knew and was moved that the words of her Old People had been recorded. When she read written sources about Ngarrindjeri history and culture, she would offer a critique in terms of what she knew from direct experience and through the stories of her Old People. For example, she had reservations about the work of Ronald and Catherine Berndt (Berndt *et al* 1993) that she voiced during the Mathews Report (1996). Kartinyeri and Anderson (2008) appeared as this book was going to press. In particular note her first hand account of reading the sources (p. 191-2) and further details of the Seven Sisters story which she now made public (p. 158).

17 See Figures 75 and 76 (Allen 2006:17–8). Blandowski's illustrations of Aboriginal people and practices from the lower southeast of South Australia are not well known in Australia. Publications and activities associated with the 150th anniversary of Blandowski's expedition to the River Murray have begun the task of popularising his work (Allen 2006).

18 Both Meyer (1846:204–5) and Berndt *et al* (1993:237–8; 453–4) recorded this story. The spider is misidentified as a tarantula which is not native to Australia.

19 At the time of going to press, the newly elected Labor Government had not radically amended the package of reforms proposed by the previous administration but had committed to a bipartisan 'war cabinet'. Hansard, http://www.aph.gov.au/hansard/hansreps.htm, February 13, 2008.

20 Appeal, February 1, 2008, to the Full Court of the Supreme Court of the decision of Gray J. in *Trevorrow v. State of South Australia*, (2007) SASC 285.

21 http://www.granniesgroup.com.au

22 http://www.au.iofc.org/Initiatives of Change IofC (formerly known as 'Moral Rearmament') is a network of people and programs committed to building trust across the world's divides. It comprises people of diverse cultures, nations, beliefs and backgrounds who are committed to transforming society through change in individuals and relationships, starting in their own lives. IofC has a long track record of working for reconciliation and understanding between Indigenous and other Australians.

23 See Birckhead *et al* 2007. This research project (a collaborative research project of Flinders University, the CSIRO and Charles Sturt University) looks at the connection between water, water-related resources and Ngarrindjeri well-being in order to provide a comprehensive overview of the value of water to the Ngarrindjeri People of the Coorong, Lower Lakes and Murray Mouth (CLLAMM), a significant ecological asset in the Living Murray program of the Murray-Darling Basin Commission (MDBC).

24 The Ngarrindjeri have established Nation to Nation relations with the Confederated Tribes of the Umatilla Indian Reservation (CTUIR) in Oregon, USA (see Rigney *et al* in press).

25 http://foundingdocs.gov.au/item.asp?dID=2

26 http://www.abc.net.au/news/newsitems/200612/s1819033.htm

27 http://www.governor.sa.gov.au/html/speeches_07/071228_proclamationday_print.html

28 Document tabled at NRA meeting Oct 13, 2007, Murray Bridge re 27/7/07 meeting to establish goals of NRA.

29 The contributions of Annie Vanderwyk to an earlier draft of this chapter are gratefully acknowledged.

30 See Editor's Epilogue p. 109-10 for a discussion of spelling Ngarrindjeri words. The spelling in brackets represents the orthography of the *Ngarrindjeri Learners' Guide* (Gale and French 2007) where it differs from the spelling used in this book.

31 The decision was appealed on February 1, 2008 to the Full Court of the South Australian Supreme Court. See note 20.

32 Gale and French (2007) provide a detailed and straightforward guide to the new orthography and outline the unique qualities of the Ngarrindjeri language. According to McDonald (2002: 19), Ngarrindjeri belongs to a group of Murray languages that share unique sound features – a five vowel system; vowel length is not crucial; a lot of interdental sounds (th, dh, nh, and lh); one of the 'r' sounds is strongly rolled; there is an extra central vowel before the retroflex (rt, rn, rl) sounds – but Ngarrindjeri alone allows some unusual consonant clusters not generally found in other Aboriginal languages.

Bibliography

Allen, Harry. (2006). Blandowski in South Australia: A consultation document prepared for Aboriginal Communities and organizations in South Australia. Auckland: Department of Anthropology, University of Auckland.

Anderson, Pat and Rex Wild. (2007). *Ampe Akelyernemane Meke Mekarle 'Little Children are Sacred'*. Report of the Board on Inquiry into the Protection of Aboriginal Children from Sexual Abuse. Northern Territory Government Australia.

Angas, George French. (1844). *Original Sketches for South Australia.* Illustrated. London: T. McLean.

____. (1847). *Savage Life and Scenes in Australia and New Zealand: Being an artist's impression of countries and people at the Antipodes.* London: Smith Elder and Co.

Atkinson, Michael. (2008a). News: Findings to be tested in the Trevorrow Appeal, February 28. http://www.ministers.sa.gov.au/news.php?id=2838

_____. (2008b) News: Attorney-General to study Trevorrow decision. February 1. http://www.ministers.sa.gov.au/news.php?id=2716

Bell, Diane. (1998). *Ngarrindjeri Wurruwarrin: A world that is, was, and will be.* Melbourne: Spinifex Press.

____. (2001). 'The word of a woman: Ngarrindjeri stories and a bridge to Hindmarsh Island'. In Peggy Brock (Ed.), *Words and Silences: Aboriginal Women, politics and land* (pp. 117-138). Sydney: Allen and Unwin.

____. (2007). 'For Aborigines? Rights and Reality'. In Neil Gillespie (Ed.), *Reflections: 40 years on from the 1967 Referendum* (pp. 97-107). Adelaide: Aboriginal Legal Rights Movement.

Berndt, Catherine H. (1994a). 'Pinkie Mack'. In David Horton (Ed.), *The Encyclopaedia of Aboriginal Australia: Aboriginal and Torres Strait Islander History, Society and Culture* (pp. 639-640). Canberra: Aboriginal Studies Press.

____. (1994b). 'Albert Karloan'. In David Horton (Ed.), *The Encyclopaedia of Aboriginal Australia: Aboriginal and Torres Strait Islander History, Society and Culture* (pp. 536-537). Canberra: Aboriginal Studies Press.

Berndt, Ronald M. (1940). 'Some aspects of Jaraldi culture, South Australia'. *Oceania*, 11 (2) pp. 164-185.

Berndt, Ronald M. and Catherine H. Berndt with John Stanton. (1993). *A World That Was: The Yaraldi of the Murray River and the Lakes, South Australia.* Melbourne: Melbourne University Press at the Miegunyah Press.

Birckhead, Jim, Romy Greiner, Steve Hemming, Daryle Rigney and the Ngarrindjeri Leadership Team (George Trevorrow, Matthew Rigney and Tom Trevorrow). (2007). Mid-project progress report. 'Water for a Healthy Country, Flagship Project: economic and cultural values of water to Indigenous People in the River Murray Region'.

Brodie, Veronica. (2007). *My Side of the Bridge: The life story of Veronica Brodie as told to Mary-Anne Gale.* Kent Town: Wakefield Press.

Brunton, Ron. (1999). Hindmarsh Island and the hoaxing of Australian anthropology. *Quadrant*, May, pp. 11-17.

Clarke, Philip A. (1994). Contact, Conflict and Regeneration: Aboriginal Cultural Geography of the Lower Murray, South Australia. Unpublished Ph.D. thesis, Department of Geography and Anthropology, University of Adelaide, South Australia.

____. (1995). Myth as history? The *Ngurunderi* dreaming of the Lower Murray, South Australia. *Records of the South Australian Museum*, 28 (2) pp. 143-156.

____. (1997). The Aboriginal cosmic landscape of southern South Australia. *Records of the South Australian Museum*, 29 (2) pp. 125-145.

Department of Education. (1990). *The Ngarrindjeri People: Aboriginal people of the River Murray, Lakes and Coorong.* Aboriginal Studies 8-12. Adelaide: Department of Education.

E.S.A. (1927). A dusky ruler. *Register*, May 11.

Fergie, Deane. (1994). To all the mothers that were, to all the mothers that are, to all the mothers that will be: An anthropological assessment of the threat of injury and desecration to Aboriginal tradition by the proposed Hindmarsh Island Bridge construction. A Report to the Aboriginal Legal Rights Movement Inc. in relation to section 10 of the *Aboriginal and Torres Strait Islander Heritage Protection Act, 1984.*

____. (1996) Secret envelopes and inferential tautologies. *Journal of Australian Studies*, 48, pp. 13-24.

Gale, Mary-Anne and Dorothy French. (2007). *Ngarrindjeri Learners' Guide* (Draft). Raukkan Community Council on behalf of the Ngarrindjeri community.

Gray, Thomas. (2007). Reasons of Decision. *Bruce Trevorrow v State of South Australia.* [2007] SASC 285.

Hemming, Steven J. (1985.) The Mulgewongk. *Journal of the Anthropological Society of South Australia,* 23 (1) pp. 11-16.

____. (1993). Camp Coorong: Combining Race Relations and Cultural Education. *Social Alternatives,* 12 (11) pp. 37-40.

____. (1994a). *Troddin thru Raukkan: Our Home: Raukkan Reunion.* Raukkan: Raukkan Council and South Australian Museum.

____. (1994b). In the tracks of *Ngurunderi*: the South Australian Museum's Ngurunderi exhibition and cultural tourism. *Australian Aboriginal Studies,* 2, pp. 38-46.

____. (1996). Inventing Ethnography. In Richard Nile and Lyndall Ryan (Eds), *Secret Women's Business: The Hindmarsh Affair, Journal of Australian Studies,* 48, pp. 25-39. St Lucia, UQP.

____. (1997). Not the slightest shred of evidence: A reply to Philip Clarke's response to 'Secret Women's Business'. *Journal of Australian Studies,* 5 (3) pp. 130-145.

____. (2006). 'The Problem with Aboriginal Heritage: Translation, Transformation and Resistance'. In G. Worby and L. I. Rigney (Eds), *Sharing Spaces: Indigenous and Non-Indigenous Responses to Story, Country and Rights.* (pp. 305-328). API Network, Perth.

Hemming, Steven J. and Philip G. Jones with Philip A. Clarke. (1989). *Ngurunderi: An Aboriginal Dreaming.* Adelaide: South Australian Museum.

Hemming, Stephen J. and Tom Trevorrow. (2005). '*Kungun Ngarrindjeri Yunnan*: archaeology, colonialism and re-claiming the future'. In Claire Smith and H. Martin Wobst (Eds) *Indigenous Archaeologies: Decolonising Theory and Practice Routledge,* (pp. 243-261). New York: Routledge.

Hemming, Steven, Daryle Rigney, Lynley Wallis, Tom Trevorrow, Matthew Rigney and George Trevorrow. (2007). Caring for Ngarrindjeri Country: Collaborative Research, Community Development and Social Justice. *Indigenous Law Bulletin,* 6 (27), 6-8.

Hemming, Steven and Chris Wilson. (in press). 'The First Stolen Generations: Repatriation and Reburial issues in perspective'. In H. Murphy and P. Turnbull (Eds), *The Long Way Home.* National Museum of Australia.

Hills, Ben. (1999). Trouble in myth business. *Sydney Morning Herald,* July 3.

Jones, Philip. (1989). 'A curve is a line and a line is a curve': Some of the truth about David Unaipon. *Adelaide Review*, 65, July, pp. 10-11.

____. (1993). David Unaipon. In John Ritchie (Ed.) *Australian Dictionary of Biography*, (pp. 303-305). Melbourne: Melbourne University Press.

Kartinyeri, Donna and Dorothy. (2007). *Pers. Comm.*

Kartinyeri, Doreen. (1983). *The Rigney Family Genealogy*. Adelaide: The Aboriginal Research Centre in the University of Adelaide.

____. (1985). *The Wanganeen Family Genealogy*. Adelaide: The Aboriginal Research Centre in the University of Adelaide.

____. (1989*). The Kartinyeri Family Genealogy*. Vols 1-2. Adelaide: South Australian Museum.

____. (1990) *The Wilson Family Genealogies*. Vols 1-3. Adelaide: South Australian Museum.

____. (1996). *Ngarrindjeri Anzacs*. Raukkan: South Australian Museum and Raukkan Council.

____. (2006) *Ngarrindjeri Nation: Genealogies of Ngarrindjeri Families*. Adelaide: Wakefield Press.

Kartinyeri, Doreen and Sue Anderson. (2008). *Doreen Kartinyeri: My Ngarrindjeri Calling*. Canberra: Aboriginal Studies Press.

Kartinyeri, Doris. (2000). *Kick the Tin*. Melbourne: Spinifex Press.

Kenny, Chris. (1996). *Women's Business*. Potts Point, NSW: Duffy and Snellgrove.

Lindsay, Rita. (2007). *Pers. Comm.*

Lindsay, Rita. (2008). *Pers. Comm.*

McKeown, Keith C. (1936). *Australian Spiders*. Sydney: Angus and Robertson.

McDonald, Maryalyce. (2002). A Study of the Phonetics and Phonology of Yaraldi and Associated Dialects. Muenchin: Lincom Europa.

Mathews, Jane. (1996). Commonwealth Hindmarsh Island Report pursuant to section 10 (4) of the *Aboriginal and Torres Strait Islander Heritage Protection Act 1984*. Canberra: Australian Government Printer.

Mattingley, Christobel and Ken Hampton. (Eds) (1988). *Survival in our own Land: Aboriginal experiences in South Australia since 1836, told by Nungas and others*. Adelaide: Wakefield Press.

Mead, Greg. (1995). *A Royal Omission*. South Australia: The Author.

Meyer, H.A.E. (1843). *Vocabulary of the Language Spoken by the Aborigines of South Australia*. Adelaide: James Allen.

____. (1846). *Manners and Customs of the Aborigines of the Encounter Bay Tribe: South Australia*. Adelaide: South Australian Government Printer. (Republished 1963, South Australian Facsimile Editions, No 20, Libraries Board of South Australia).

Muecke, Stephen and Adam Shoemaker. (Eds) (2001). *Legendary Tales of the Australian Aborigines, David Unaipon*. Melbourne University Press at the Miegunyah Press.

Ngarrindjeri Regional Authority. (2008). Networking the Ngarrindjeri: A regional approach to communications to link Indigenous enterprises in the Lower Murray, Lakes and Coorong. Prebudget Submission to the Office of the Treasurer, Canberra, ACT, Australia. January 16.

Ngarrindjeri Tendi, Ngarrindjeri Heritage Committee, Ngarrindjeri Native Title Management Committee. (2006). *Ngarrindjeri Nation Yarluwar-Ruwe Plan*: Caring for Ngarrindjeri Sea Country and Culture. Meningie: NLPA.

Pearson, Christopher. (1998). A twist in the tale: yarns and symbols. *Australian Financial Review*. August 17.

Penney, Richard (aka: 'Cuique'). (1842). The Spirit of the Murray. *South Australian Magazine*. June-July. Reprinted in the *Journal of Anthropological Society of South Australia*, 29, (1) 1991, pp. 1-87 (with an introduction by Robert Foster).

Rankine, Annie. (1969). *Old ways and new*. Ms No. 1439, recorder unknown, 11/3/1969. Canberra: Australian Institute of Aboriginal and Torres Strait Islander Studies.

Rankine, Leila. (1974). Pattern of Human Life on the Murray Pre-1850: The actual present. Lecture given at the Goolwa Seminar, University of Adelaide, January 10.

Rankine, Leila. (c1980). *Poems*. Adelaide: Self Published.

Rann, Mike. (2007). News: Bruce Trevorrow will get full compensation. http://www.ministers.sa.gov.au/news.php?id=1963

Rigney, Daryle, Steve Hemming and Shaun Berg. (in press). 'Letters patent, native title and the Crown in South Australia'. In Daryle Rigney, Martin Hinton and Elliott Johnston (Eds), *Indigenous Australians and the Law* (2nd edition). Sydney: Routledge-Cavendish.

Rudd, Kevin. (2008). Apology to Australia's Indigenous Peoples. Votes and

Proceedings. *Hansard*. p. 1. House of Representatives. Commonwealth of Australia, Wednesday 13 February.

Saunders, Cheryl. (1994). Report to the Minister for Aboriginal and Torres Strait Islander Affairs on the significant Aboriginal area in the vicinity of Goolwa and Hindmarsh (*Kumarangk*) Island. Adelaide: South Australian Government Printer.

Simons, Margaret. (2003). *The Meeting of the Waters: The Hindmarsh Island Affair*. Sydney: Hodder.

Smith, W. Ramsay. (1930). *Myths and Legends of the Australian Aboriginals*. London: Harrap.

Stevens, Iris. (1995). *Report of the Hindmarsh Island Bridge Royal Commission*. Adelaide: South Australian Government Printer.

Sturt, Charles. (1833). *Two Expeditions into the Interior of Southern Australia*. Two volumes. London: Smith, Elder and Co.

Taplin, George. (1859-79). Journal: Five volumes as typed from the original by Mrs Beaumount. Adelaide: Mortlock Library.

____. (1873). The Narrinyeri. Reprinted in J.D.Woods (Ed.), *The Native Tribes of South Australia* (pp. 1-156). Adelaide: E.S. Wigg & Son.

____. (1878). *Grammar of the Language of the "Narrinyeri" Tribe*. Adelaide: South Australian Government Printer.

____. (1879). *Folklore, Manners and Customs of the South Australian Aborigines: Gathered from inquiries made by authority of the South Australian government*. Adelaide: E. Spiller, Acting Government Printer.

Taylor, Kaysha. (2007). *Pers. Comm.*

Tindale, Norman B. (1931-4). *Journal of Researches in the South East of South Australia*, 1. Adelaide: Anthropology Archives. South Australian Museum.

____. (1938). Prupe and Koromarange: A Legend of the Tanganekald, Coorong, South Australia. *Transactions of the Royal Society of South Australia*, 62: 18-23.

____. (1986). Milerum. In Bede Nairn and Geoffrey Serle (Eds), *Australian Dictionary of Biography*, 11, *1891-1939*. (pp. 498-9). Melbourne: Melbourne University Press.

____. (nd). Anthropology Archive. Adelaide: South Australian Museum.

Tindale, Norman B. and Clarence Long. (nd). The World of Milerum. Stage A, volumes 1-10. Adelaide: Anthropology Archive: South Australian Museum.

Treagus, Elaine. (1966). Archive Tape, LA 3462A. Canberra: Australian Institute of Aboriginal and Torres Strait Islander Studies.

Trevorrow, Georgie. (2007). *Pers. Comm.*

Trevorrow, Tom, Christine Finnimore, Steven Hemming, George Trevorrow, Matthew Rigney, Veronica Brodie and Ellen Trevorrow. (2007). *They took our land and then our children.* Meningie: Ngarrindjeri Lands and Progress Association.

Unaipon, David. (1924-5). *Legendary Tales of the Australian Aborigines.* MS copy (MLA 1929 Cyreel 1134). Sydney: Mitchell Library.

____. (1925). The story of the *Mungingee. The Home*, February, pp. 42-3.

____. (1990). *Narroondarie's* wives. In Jack Davies, Stephen Muecke, Mudrooroo Narogin and Adam Shoemaker (Eds) *Paperbark: A collection of Black Australia Writing.* (pp. 19-32). St Lucia: University of Queensland Press.

von Doussa, John (2001). Reasons for Decision. *Thomas Lincoln Chapman and Ors v Luminis Pty Ltd, 088 127 085 and Ors, Federal Court of Australia*, No. SG 33 OF 1997.

Wallis, L., Hemming, S., Wilson, C. (2006). The *Warnung* (Hack's Point) Old People's Place Project: A collaborative approach to archaeological survey, research and management planning, Report Prepared for the Ngarrindjeri Heritage Committee, Ngarrindjeri Native Title Management Committee and Ngarrindjeri Tendi.

Wilson, Chris. (2005). Returning of the Ngarrindjeri: Repatriating Old People Back to Country, BA Honours thesis in Archaeology, Flinders University.

Wilson, Dulcie. (1998). *The Cost of Crossing Bridges.* Mitcham: Small Poppy Publishing.

Wilson, Ronald (Sir). (1997). *Bringing Them Home: Report of the National Inquiry into the Separation of Aboriginal and Torres Strait Islander Children from their Families.* Sydney: Human Rights and Equal Opportunity Commission.

Yallop, Collin and G. Grimwade. (1975). *Narinjari: An outline of the language studied by George Taplin, with Taplin's Notes and comparative table. Language 1864-1964.* Oceania Linguistic Monograph (17), Sydney.

Cases

Kartinyeri & Anor v. Commonwealth ('*Hindmarsh Island Bridge* case') (1998) 195 CLR 337.

Chapman v. Tickner and others (1995) 55 FCR 316.

Tickner v *Chapman* (1995) 133 ALR 226.

Tickner v *Western Australia* (Full Federal Court, unreported, May 28 1996); see Nathan Hancock, 'Casenote', *Aboriginal Law Bulletin* 3, no. 82 (1996): 12-13.

Wilson v *Minister for Aboriginal and Torres Strait Islander Affairs* (1996) 189 CLR 1.

Appeal, February 1, 2008, to the Full Court of the Supreme Court of the decision of Gray J. in Trevorrow v. State of South Australia, (2007) SASC 285.

Bruce Trevorrow v State of South Australia. [2007] SASC 285.

Thomas Lincoln Chapman and Ors v Luminis Pty Ltd, 088 127 085 and Ors, Federal Court of Australia, No. SG 33 OF 1997.

Name Index

General Index

About the Authors

Ngarrindjeri Lands and Progress Association

The Ngarrindjeri Lands and Progress Association (NLPA) was established by Meningie Ngarrindjeri people in 1985 to further Ngarrindjeri interests in cultural heritage, language, arts, education and Ngarrindjeri lands and waters. The NLPA runs the Camp Coorong: Race Relations and Cultural Education Centre and the Camp Coorong Museum as places where people, Indigenous and non-Indigenous, can learn about Ngarrindjeri heritage and culture. Camp Coorong offers basket weaving and story-telling workshops, organises field trips through their country and has had enormous success with the educational programs that cater for groups from local school children to international tour groups. Over the past seven years, the NLPA has also sponsored and mentored a number of university students whose research degrees focus on Ngarrindjeri history and culture. Ngarrindjeri organisations have been keen to partner with educational and research institutions and to publish their findings. Partners include Flinders University, University of Adelaide, University of South Australia, CSIRO, South Australian Museum, Migration Museum, and the Department of Education, SA. This is NLPA's first joint publication with a trade publisher.

NLPA supported publications include

Ngurunderi exhibition (1989–1999), film and book (1989)

Troddin Thru Raukkan, our home: Raukkan reunion (1994)

Ngarrindjeri Fruits and Medicine Plants (2006)

Ngarrindjeri Nation Yarluwar-Ruwe Plan: Caring for Ngarrindjeri Sea Country and Culture (2006)

They Took Our Land and Then They Took Our Children (2007)

Diane Bell

Diane Bell is Professor Emerita of Anthropology, The George Washington University, DC, USA; Professor of Anthropology, University of Adelaide; Writer and Editor in Residence, Flinders University. Her research has focussed on the rights of Indigenous women, Indigenous land rights, human rights, Indigenous religions, violence against women, the writing of feminist ethnography and environmental issues. After a distinguished career in Australia and the USA, she has retired to Ngarrindjeri country in South Australia where she continues to research, write and strategise around issues of local, national and international importance.

Ellen Trevorrow and Diane Bell,
Camp Coorong, October 2, 2007

Photograph: Vesper Tjukonai

Other books by Diane Bell
    Law: the Old and The New (co-author, 1980, 1984)
    Daughters of the Dreaming (1983, 1993, 2002)
    Religion in Aboriginal Australia (co-editor, 1984)
    Generations: Grandmothers, mothers and daughters (1987)
    Longman's Encyclopaedia (joint editor, 1989)
    Gendered Fields: Women, men and ethnography (co-editor 1993)
    Radically Speaking: Feminism reclaimed (co-editor 1996)
    Ngarrindjeri Wurruwarrin: A world that is, was, and will be (1998)
    Evil: A novel (2005)

Electronic Publications
    All about Water: All about the River (co-edited 2007)

Appendix 1

Apology of the Alexandrina Council, October 8, 2002

Sincere expression of sorrow and apology to the Ngarrindjeri People

To the Ngarrindjeri people, the traditional owners of the land and waters within the region, the Alexandrina Council expresses sorrow and sincere regret for the suffering and injustice that you have experienced since colonisation and we share with you our feelings of shame and sorrow at the mistreatment your people have suffered.

We respect your autonomy and uniqueness of your culture. We offer our support and commitment to your determination to empower your communities in the struggle for justice, freedom and protection of your Heritage, Culture and interests within the Council area and acknowledge your right to determine your future.

We commit to work with you. We acknowledge your wisdom and we commit to ensuring our actions and expressions best assist your work. We accept your frustrations at our past ways of misunderstanding you.

We are shamed to acknowledge that there is still racism within our communities. We accept that our words must match our actions and we pledge to you that we will work to remove racism and ignorance.

We will recognise your leadership, we honour your visions, and we hope for a future of working together with respect for each other.

We look forward to achieving reconciliation with justice.

We ask to walk beside you, and to stand with you to remedy the legacy of 166 years of European occupation of your land and waters and control of your lives.

The work of the Alexandrina Council will be guided by your vision of a future where reconciliation through agreement making may be possible and we may walk together.

The Alexandrina Council acknowledges the Ngarrindjeri People's ongoing connection to the land and waters within its area and further acknowledges the Ngarrindjeri People's continuing culture and interests therein.

Signed for and on behalf of the Alexandrina Council by Mayor
Mr Kym McHugh

Witnessed for the Council by the Chief Executive,
Mr John Coombe

Witnessed for the Ngarrindjeri People by the Rupelle of the Ngarrindjeri Tendi,
Mr George Trevorrow

Witnessed for Ngarrindjeri People by the Chair of Ngarrindjeri Native Title Committee
Mr Matthew Rigney

Witnessed for the Ngarrindjeri People by the Chair of Ngarrindjeri Heritage Committee
Mr Tom Trevorrow

ALEXANDRINA COUNCIL   ABN 20 785 405 351   Preserving the Past – Securing the Future

Postal Address: Post Office Box 21 Goolwa SA 5214 **Telephone** (08) 8555 7000 **Facsimile** (08) 8555 3603
16 Dawson Street Goolwa Email alex@alexandrina.sa.gov.au 1 Colman Terrace Strathalbyn
Web www.alexandrina.sa.gov.au

Appendix 2

Proclamation of Ngarrindjeri Dominium, December 17, 2003

Proclamation of Ngarrindjeri Dominium

This proclamation was hand delivered to
Her Excellency Marjorie Jackson Nelson, Governor of South Australia,
by four Ngarrindjeri leaders,
George Trevorrow, Matt Rigney, Tom Trevorrow amd Ellen Trevorrow
on the 17th December 2003
for presentation to the State Government.

PROCLAMATION of
The time immemorial Ngarrindjeri Dominium

Now Being First Notified to

Her Excellency, Marjorie Jackson-Nelson. Governor of South Australia
FOR THE CROWN IN THE RIGHT OF THE STATE OF SOUTH AUSTRALIA
AS REPRESENTED BY EXECUTIVE COUNCIL
FOR AND ON BEHALF OF THE INHABITANTS OF SOUTH AUSTRALIA

Greetings!

1. WHEREAS by statute assented to in 1834 the Crown of the United Kingdom of Great Britain proposed to declare certain lands wrongly presumed by Preamble to be "*waste and unoccupied*" in a "*province of South Australia*" to be established without notice to its Indigenous inhabitant proprietors, to be "*open to purchase by British subjects*" upon its establishment [s.6, South Australia Act 4&5 William IV, cap.95,]; and,

2. WHEREAS in December 1835 at London, the South Australian Colonizing Commission denied on behalf of the promoters of the said Province "*this declaration of the legislature as absolutely rebutting, the title of any aboriginal inhabitants of the proposed Colony to the occupation of the Soil*" [C.O.13/3]; and,

3. WHEREAS on 6 January 1836 at London, the South Australian Colonizing Commission agreed to submit "*arrangements for purchasing the lands of the natives*" of "*the province of South Australia*" to the Colonial Office at the request by letter of the Secretary of State for the Colonies, Lord Glenelg; and,

4. WHEREAS in their First Report to the Parliament of the said United Kingdom the South Australian Colonizing Commission agreed that "*the locations of the colonists will be conducted on the principle of securing to the natives [sic] their proprietary right to the soil'- so as to require cession of any territory to be "perfectly voluntary*"

[First Annual Report of the South Australian Colonizing Commissioners, House of Commons, 1836 Sessional Papers 36 No. 491, 39 No.426, pp. 8-9]; and,

5. WHEREAS the said arrangements proposed that the Crown of the United Kingdom of Great Britain allow the opening for public sale in England of "*those lands uninhabited or not in the occupation and enjoyment of the Native race*" in "*the province of South Australia*"; and

6. WHEREAS the said arrangements proposed that

"*should the Natives occupying or enjoying any lands comprised within the surveys directed by the Colonial Commissioner not surrender their right to such lands by a voluntary sale*";

Then in that case the Colonizing Commissioners have two duties, namely:

ONE [The first Duty]

"*to **secure** to the Natives the full and undisturbed occupation or enjoyment of those lands*",

and TWO [The Second Duty]

"*to afford them **legal redress** against depredations and **trespasses**"*; and,

7. WHEREAS by Letters Patent of 1836 issued to Governor Hindmarsh in London the Crown of the United Kingdom of Great Britain purported to allow the said Colonizing Commissioner to begin embarking British subjects upon certain commercial terms on ships and sail for South Australia on condition

'*that nothing in these Letters Patent contained shall effect or be construed to effect the **rights** of any aboriginal Natives of the said province to the actual **occupation** or enjoyment in their persons or in the persons of their **descendants** of any lands now actually occupied or enjoyed by such Natives*" [C.O. 13/3]; and,

8. WHEREAS clause 34 of the Instruction to the Resident Colonizing Commissioner guaranteed that

"*no lands which the natives may possess in occupation or enjoyment be offered for sale until previously **ceded** by the natives*"

[The Select Committee on the Aborigines, Report, 19 September 1860, Legislative Council of the Parliament of South Australia, p.5]; and,

9. WHEREAS clause 35 of the said Instructions to the Resident Colonizing Commissioner required that

"*the aborigines are **not disturbed** in the enjoyment of the lands over which they may possess proprietary rights, and of which they are not disposed to make a voluntary sale*" and required "*evidence of the faithful fulfillment of the bargains or **treaties** which you may effect with the aborigines for the cessation of lands*"

[op.cit.]; and,

BEING APPRISED OF THE INEQUITY WE THEREUPON SUFFER, TAKE NOTICE THAT:

The fundamental relationship between the governed and government in South Australia has never been achieved in a politically democratic, equal and just process over the life of the State, because Aboriginal people lack due Constitutional recognition for their original land rights in the State.

The Constitution of the Parliament of South Australia was drafted by a 19th Century Premier of South Australia, without the full democratic involvement of the people or the community, and without Aboriginal input.

Of main concern for the better future of South Australia is the just, equal and democratic treatment of all South Australians by government, and especially of all Aboriginal people, and in recognition of their prior equity.

At the heart of the principle of a social contract between the people and Government is the right of the community to determine its future by making society accountable to the State, within a just system of laws.

South Australia began in an 1834 Act of a colonising British Parliament in London half-way around the world, and it determined all local Aboriginal people to be *persona nullius*, despite their inherent proprietary rights.

The founding legislation for South Australia was an ignominious start to a 167 year history of infamy for the Aboriginal people, who have never been asked to establish any form of legal relations with the colonising state.

Central to the Wakefield Plan for colonising the Aboriginal lands of South Australia was a repugnance for slavery and securing of a privileged English social contract for a few, while dispossessing Aboriginal land owners.

Slavery had been abolished in Britain and its colonies from 1833, and the worst fear of the emigrants to South Australia was being found guilty of enslaving the Aboriginal people. To avoid any legal penalty for slavery and to avoid any allegation of slavery, Aboriginal people were deprived of any right or equity to their lands and were refused the social right to work.

This was a specific design especially incorporated in the establishment of South Australia. Although Aboriginal people were British subjects by law, this was only nominal justice, because taking their lands was justified.

The legal doctrine of *terra nullius* refuted by the Mabo judgment was developed by English law to permanently entrench this injustice in the State's legal and constitutional framework, and to deny Aboriginal equity.

There is an urgent need for the people of South Australia to recognise this ignominy of the past and to go forward together with all the local Aboriginal people for a better and more just future in community upholding respect.

It is up to the community to extend the hand of partnership and co-operation to all people and groups in the State, and to reform South Australia to be inclusive of everyone's rights.

The traditional way to achieve unison of this nature, both for Indigenous and immigrant cultures alike, is for a social compact or contract to be formulated to establish the peace.

The whole community must be consulted and all interest groups must have a legal right to negotiate with government in the make-up and terms of a rewrite of the State's Constitution.

A bright and just future for all is only based upon an equal and democratic negotiation by all.

Accordingly, as -

THE NGARRINDJERI HAVE ALWAYS **OCCUPIED** THE TRADITIONAL LANDS OF THE NGARRINDJERI NATION

and

NGARRINDJERI HAVE NEVER **CEDED** NOR SOLD OUR LANDS AND WATERS,

We ambassadors of the Ngarrindjeri Nation, George Trevorrow, Rupelli of the Ngarrindjeri Tendi, Thomas Edwin Trevorrow, Chairperson of the Ngarrindjeri Heritage Committee, and Matt Rigney, Chairperson of the Ngarrindjeri Native Title Committee, having been properly authorised in the Ngarrindjeri way to make this proclamation on behalf of all Ngarrindjeri, do hereby:

declare and proclaim

our homeland as traditionally delineated, including all waters, foreshore and riverbed thereof,

is now and always has been occupied by Ngarrindjeri.

THEREFORE WE HUMBLY REQUIRE THAT YOUR CROWN
FORTHWITH RECOGNISE THE NGARRINDJERI DOMINIUM IN OUR
SOIL AND BENEATH OUR WATERS, AS IS OUR ORIGINAL RIGHT AND
DOMINION EVIDENCED BY OUR NATIVE RIGHT, AND -

ONE:

**Enter a Social Charter with the Ngarrindjeri Nation to inscribe the mutual
recognition of our dominium as between the Ngarrindjeri Nation and the
Crown within South Australia;**
and

TWO:

Present Parliament with a Bill for a Ngarrindjeri treaty to be enacted by
indenture, which secures the Dominium of our Ngarrindjeri lands and waters to
the perpetual inheritance of the Ngarrindjeri Nation, and which enshrines a Bill
of Rights for the advancement of the human rights of all South Australians, and
the particular maintenance of the Ngarrindjeri heritage in perpetuity.

Given under our hand and the Public Seal of Ngarrindjeri
as presented to the Governor of South Australia on Wednesday the 17th day of
December 2003.

SIGNED: ....
George Trevorrow, Rupelli of the Ngarrindjeri Tendi

....
Thomas Edwin Trevorrow, Chairperson of the Ngarrindjeri Heritage
Committee

....
Matt Rigney, Chairperson of the Ngarrindjeri Native Title
Committee

Recorded in Register of Ngarrindjeri Proclamations, Vol 2, Page 1

Copies transmitted this day to

The Governor of South Australia [the Representative of the Crown, acting with
the advice and consent of the Executive Council].

Her Majesty Queen Elizabeth II, Queen of Australia and the United Kingdom of
Great Britain and Northern Ireland.

The Ngarrindjeri Nation calls on the S.A. Government to meet with
the Ngarrindjeri leaders and Elders to negotiate a Treaty between both
governments.

If you would like to know more about Spinifex Press,
write for a free catalogue or visit our website.

SPINIFEX PRESS

PO Box 212, North Melbourne
Victoria 3051, Australia
www.spinifexpress.com.au

Many Spinifex books are now also available as eBooks.
See the eBookstore on our website for more details.